BY
STEPHEN M. POLLAN

MARK LEVINE
AND
MICHAEL POLLAN

A Fireside Book
Published by Simon & Schuster Inc.
New York   London   Toronto   Sydney   Tokyo

THE
FIELD
GUIDE
TO
HOME
BUYING
IN
AMERICA

A Home Buyer's Companion from
House Hunting to Moving Day

Published by Simon & Schuster Inc.
Simon & Schuster Building
Rockefeller Center
1230 Avenue of the Americas
New York, New York 10020
FIRESIDE and colophon are registered
trademarks of Simon & Schuster Inc.
Designed by Lynne Kopcik/Barbara Marks
Manufactured in the United States of America
10   9   8   7   6   5

Library of Congress Cataloging in Publication Data

Pollan, Stephen M.
    The field guide to home buying in America: a home buyer's
companion from house hunting to moving day / by Stephen M.
Pollan, Michael Pollan, and Mark Levine.
        p.   cm.
    "A Fireside book."
    Includes index.
    1. House   buying.   I. Pollan,   Michael.   II. Levine,   Mark.
        III. Title.
HD1379.P63 1988   88-6626
643'.12—dc19   CIP

ISBN 0-671-63961-7

ACKNOWLEDGMENTS

The authors would like to express gratitude to the following individuals for their creative input, editorial assistance and research endeavors in the preparation of this book: Shannon Carney, Jane Morrow, Angela Paura, Victoria Pesce, Gregor Roy and Lisa Schneiderman.

In addition, a special note of thanks is due to Freda Levine and Deirdre Martin for their continual support and encouragement.

We would like to express our appreciation to Roberta Pryor, who helped to inspire the entire project.

This book is dedicated to the memory of Tim McGinnis, whose enthusiasm, intelligence and warmth were so much a part of the project. He will be sorely missed.

CONTENTS

CONTENTS

PREFACE

Over the past thirty years, I have taken part in the purchase of hundreds of homes—a handful of my own, several by my children and parents and scores of others by my clients. In all of these transactions I have been struck by what a large part fear and self-doubt play in the home-buying process. Whether it is a young couple starting out, a seasoned investor, an heir for whom money is no object, crippling uncertainties crop up: Am I overcommiting myself financially? Do I really want to put down roots here? Am I paying too much? Have I made a mistake?

All these fears are completely understandable—and all can be overcome.

Purchase of a home is certainly a momentous occasion, but it also be a joyous one. Buying a home is one of the few actions we can take that can simultaneously enhance both the financial and spiritual dimensions of our lives. It can start us on the road to financial security and growth, and it can give an unmatched stability to our lives and our family. Home ownership can be profoundly rewarding.

So why all the fear? Some of it stems from the large amounts of money involved, apart from the reluctance many of us have to commit ourselves. I am convinced that the greatest obstacle to the first-time home buyer is the lack of sound guidance and support he or she typically faces. There is never any shortage of advice offered—lawyers, brokers, bankers, accountants. Most of these actors have their own interests at heart, and while one might have good legal advice and the other can tell you something about the housing market or the mortgage scene, there is never anyone who can pull it all together, help you see the whole picture, and then provide the emotional support most of us need to get through the home-buying process. A home buyer's ideal adviser combines the skills and perspective of lawyer, accountant, broker, banker, diplomat, friend and psychiatrist.

Insofar as it is possible, I try to combine all these roles in my practice. I am, by training, a lawyer. I have also been a broker, banker and financial adviser, and while I have never practiced psychiatry, I know from long firsthand experience all the complicated emotions that invariably accompany the making of a big financial commitment or the conduct of a tense negotiation.

I have discovered that there is an astonishing demand for the service of an adviser who can walk someone through the entire home-buying process, from the first decisions about budget and location all the way to the closing. This is particularly true among first-time buyers today, who encounter a very different (and considerably more challenging) situation than their parents did. Baby boomers face a new set of rules. For example, "saving up" to buy a home is no longer necessarily the best route. It may make more sense to borrow the down payment from your parents. That's why some of the more delicate negotiations I conduct are not between buyer and seller, but between children and their parents. There is nothing cut-and-dried about the home-buying process today.

What I have attempted in writing this *Field Guide to Home Buying* is to translate what I do in my practice to the pages of this book. That doesn't mean that the book should take the place of competent professional advice. As you'll see in the coming chapters, I am a firm believer in the use of experts. But no single expert is likely to help you keep the whole picture in view—or tell you how to handle the experts. That's where I come in.

This book differs from others you may have read on the subject in that it tells you what to do at each stage in the process. While it is chock-full of information, it is not so much a textbook or encyclopedia as it is a home buyer's companion. Here, you'll find facts and figures balanced by advice, information tempered by experience. Each step of the way I have tried to arm you not only with the facts you will want, but also the tactics and attitudes you'll need to achieve your objectives.

The advice you'll find in the following chapters is not particularly elaborate or arcane. There are no trick deals or "power negotiating strategies" revealed in these pages. What I have to offer, by and large, is common sense, borne of my thirty years of experience. But I think you'll discover that, in the midst of the home-buying process, common sense can prove uncommonly powerful. It will help you figure out what you want, and tell you how to get it. It will dispel your fears and uncertainties, and turn an intimidating event into a joyous one.

Stephen Pollan

CHAPTER ONE

TAKING CHARGE OF THE REAL ESTATE PURCHASE

Ah, but a man's reach should exceed his grasp, Or what's a heaven for?
ROBERT BROWNING

The desire to own one's home cuts across cultural, ethnic and historical barriers. There is a measure of stability in owning a home, in the attachment to the earth it brings. It is something that all of us instinctively cherish.

The sale of a home takes on spiritual overtones—for both the buyer and seller. Often, the home has become a family museum for the sellers, who see the sale as the close of a wonderful chapter in their lives. The buyers see the purchase of a home—a home they may already have fallen in love with—as the beginning of a new chapter in their lives; and beginnings are always filled with great expectations, as well as a certain amount of fear.

Despite the seemingly inflated prices of homes in today's market, there has never been a better climate for buying—the tools for doing so have never been so plentiful or so widely available.

Today, banks are churning out mortgage money at an unprecedented rate. They have also abandoned their preconceived notions about who can own a home. Where at one time young married couples predominated, a new constituency of home buyers has emerged—singles, unmarried couples, senior citizens. These days, if your eyes are clear and there is blood running through your veins, a bank will give you a mortgage. The strict policies and formulas traditionally applied to judge affordability no longer rule. Today, underwriters are only concerned with the bottom line: your ability to pay back the loan. And if you can line up someone to guarantee your mortgage, the bank won't even care about your ability to pay back.

In addition, high prices have been answered by changes in the market—in particular the emergence of the co-op and condo—which make homes more affordable by situating them more densely. The suburban development ranch home of the fifties and sixties is now the condo near the urban center.

Buyers are coping with the upward pricing spiral by their willingness to sacrifice more for their dream house. People are starting smaller, cutting down on visits to the hairdresser, eating home more often, buying clothes every other season—all in an effort to extend their home-buying reach. And then they reach a bit further still in order to realize their dream.

Contrary to what you may have read, the new tax law actually reinforces the financial advantages of home ownership. Owning your own shelter has always been the most wonderful tax shelter there is. At present, for many Americans, it's one of the *few* tax shelters left.

Today, astute financial advisers will steer clients toward buying a home as early in their lives as possible. In over thirty years of advising people about real estate and finance, I have found that, while it is always a struggle in the first year, magical things begin to happen for people with a sense of urgency and persistence. After working through several recessions and periods of inflation, I have found that, although there are good and bad times to sell a home, there is never a bad time to buy one.

The home isn't just a place for body and soul. It's the ultimate retirement asset, the source of children's college tuition, the asset that can always be borrowed against in case of emergency. Though the stock market may rise again meteorically, and interest rates may climb, the only asset I can truly be sure of are my personal real estate holdings. I cannot control the companies in which I own stock. I don't sit on the Federal Reserve Board and dictate interest rates. But I can control my real estate. God no longer makes land, yet He continues to make people, and as a consequence real estate continues to rise in value.

Real estate remains a hedge against inflation, historically growing in value at a higher rate than the cost of living. And it is one of the few financial areas where the average American can exploit the benefits of *leverage*—your $10,000 down payment on a $100,000 home appreciates as if it were $100,000. You will be paying the lender back with cheaper dollars shrunk by inflation, while the value of the home you bought almost invariably increases. Real estate is often our only chance to begin a career of asset acquisition, and can be the first step in creating a net worth. While the new tax law does diminish some of the advantages of home ownership, the clear-cut advantages over renting remain. The "taxable event"—the sale of your home at a profit—is still deferred, as in the past, provided the money is reinvested in another home within two years of the sale. A large portion of your mortgage payment is still tax deductible during the early years. While the initial costs of ownership are greater than renting, the home owner will pay less than the tenant over the long term. And if you sell your home at age fifty-five or older, the first $125,000 of profit is tax free.

But beyond all the financial benefits, the fundamental advantages of owning a home are the security, satisfaction and pleasure it affords you. Most so-called real estate experts flip the priorities, placing the emphasis on the investment. But it is the gratification of owning and living in your own wonderful space that is the principle benefit of buying a home. Once you do own your own home you'll be hard pressed to imagine how you did without it before. You'll wonder how you could have gotten by without all that storage space, or that extra bedroom that became your home office. And how did you ever get along without a deck or a view?

The real estate market, like all others, is subject to the pyschological tremors that Black Monday—the stock market's October 1987 crash—sent through the financial world. When there is fear of the future, consumer purchases, in general, are down.

But that doesn't mean you shouldn't buy a home. Short term fears and predictions by financial prognosticators shouldn't deter you from making a long-term safe investment in a home. Mortgage rates surely are affected by financial tremors, and shifts in the rates may affect your affordability, but they should not keep you from buying. Instead, reformulate your purchase, perhaps by putting down more cash, or reassessing how much you can spend.

Whatever lessons Black Monday may hold, it convinces me once again that for the long haul, real estate is still the best investment around.

Home ownership isn't merely the acquisition of an asset. It helps us grow and mature as individuals. It seasons us and better prepares us for life. It is a phenomenal journey that leads not only to a sounder financial footing, but also to a more powerful understanding of our own abilities. I have seen my own children—all of whom bought homes before they were thirty years old and before they were married—turn into better business people and better managers of the other financial aspects of their lives as a result. It has accelerated their maturity and given them a worldliness they never had before. Home ownership doesn't make you old before your time, or tie you down to one place. It actually gives you a "leg up" on life.

I have seen clients of mine who in middle age decided to buy a new home, and by so doing, renewed and reinvigorated their lives. I've seen the purchase of a home improve relationships—the common struggle firming up otherwise shaky partnerships. While it's no antidote for divorce, the joint goals and struggles involved in home ownership can help to unite two people.

But have no illusions. There *are* some disadvantages to owning a home. For example, you are responsible for the maintenance of your home—there's no super or landlord to call if the toilet backs up or the faucet leaks. As a home owner you will have less mobility than a renter. Since the most affordable homes tend to be farther from the urban center than rental apartments, your travel time to and from work is likely to be longer once you've bought a home. Owning a home means having to deal with increases in utilities and other expenses directly, rather than indirectly through rent increases. The mortgage is a large financial obligation for a long period of time—probably the largest financial obligation you are ever likely to incur. And it is possible to make a mistake.

All these burdens are real and often substantial. But they are not really disadvantages. They actually are fears—very natural ones, but nonetheless fears which can be dispelled if closely examined.

The costs are far outweighed by the financial benefits that come from owning a home. You are not investing your money in a frozen asset; your investment almost invariably grows in value. Today, the mortgage must be viewed not as a thirty-year ball-and-chain, but rather as just one more monthly living expense. The mortgage will also become a tool for your financial future. Second mortgages, secured by the equity you have built up in your home, are no longer regarded as the last gasp of a financially strapped loser, but rather as an astute financial maneuver. Congress has even preserved the tax deductions on second mortgages in many cases. Though they should never be viewed as a financial panacea, they offer an opportunity for you to exploit the same powerful financial tool that real estate professionals have had at their disposal for years.

In addition, the ownership of a home brings with it a deeper sense and awareness of your environment than you have ever had before. Once you begin paying taxes for a school system, a fire department, a parks and recreation department, you'll find yourself developing a concern for your surroundings that you've never had before. You'll be more conscious of local government and its actions. An interesting, exciting new window on the world will open up for you.

Today's astute real estate owners often regret the expiration of their mortgages or the sale of their homes. Many take out another mortgage on the home in order to have the use of the wealth their home represents without giving up the deed. Land is so precious that some owners refuse to part with the deed. In places such as Hawaii, Hong Kong, and Nassau County on Long Island, where land is not only expensive, but in extremely short supply, sales of land are becoming rare— long-term leases are the norm. Instead of looking forward to the day when we can burn the mortgage in celebration, today we view it as a support, as a key financial tool in the course of our lives.

Is loss of mobility really such a problem? First, if your career forces you to relocate, you can always sell your home. It may take a few months, but that only means you will have to do a little planning ahead. Besides, many large companies have relocation services to help you sell and buy homes.

And if you have to leave before the house is sold, that's okay too. You can usually borrow against the equity in the first home to make a down payment on a new one—such *bridge loans* are an interesting logistical issue that we will discuss later in this book. The ability to buy and sell simultaneously has become more important in today's changing economic environment.

Second, if you are worried about being tied to one geographic area and think that your lot in life will improve simply because you are free to change your mailing address frequently, you've got some psychological problems that can't be solved by buying a home. The city you are in, the job you have, the place you live, are not responsible for your happiness or unhappiness. *You* are. Wherever you go, however often you move, you take your personal baggage with you. Ownership of a home won't clear up your private problems but neither will it add new ones.

If you are excessively worried about not being able to make your payments and having the bank foreclose on your mortgage, you're never going to buy a home. Yes, if you lose your job and miss too many mortgage payments you will lose your home. And if you get hit by lightning you'll probably die. You can't plan for every disaster. If you dwell on all the negative things that can happen to you you'll never do anything. Besides, the foreclosure rate is way down today— under 2 percent. The last thing the bank wants is your home. They want you to pay back the loan and will work with you if any problems develop. In fact, the bank will be more understanding than your credit card company, and is more likely to help you work things out than your maiden aunt would be if you owed her money.

Foreclosure has become very complicated today. This is due to the secondary mortgage market—since the banker to whom you make your monthly payments is probably only a funds collector and doesn't even hold the mortgage anymore. Bankers have a great deal of freedom to make deals and arrangements that will avoid foreclosure. A landlord would throw you out on the street a lot faster than the bank would. My personal experience as a banker has taught me that the people in a bank's mortgage department are the best, most caring bank personnel around. They are usually in the higher echelon, and as such are more understanding individuals— willing to deal with you as an individual, thanks to their own experience and confidence.

Another big fear is the fear of making a mistake, such as buying a home that doesn't increase in value, or one that turns into a bottomless money pit. A poor purchase can be a major problem, but this book will ensure that you don't make such a bad buy. I'll tell you how to check out the neighborhood and spot signs of deterioration. I'll also teach you how to evaluate the homes you're thinking of buying, and then how to work with professional inspectors and engineers to make sure that you are made aware of all the hidden costs in the home.

Now there's a trick to dispelling your fears: Keep in mind that you are not buying a home to last the next thirty years. This will undoubtedly not be the only home you ever live in. Most Americans buy a new home every seven years—just about the time the new appliances start to wear out. No home is ever going to be perfect for you. But you needn't look for perfection. Just look for a home that meets your current and short-term needs. You are looking for home number one. When you outgrow it you'll be looking for home number two. And then, perhaps after the children have left the nest, you'll go on to look for home number three. Somewhere along the way you may even buy a summer house. If you don't look for perfection you won't fear making a permanent mistake. No home is a glass slipper, a perfect fit. Sometimes you have to squeeze into a home. Other times you have to grow into it.

Another underlying fear for most of us is the fear of change. The thought of buying a home is frightening, to invest more money than you've ever had before in a single place—and a place that may not be perfect. But once you understand the process, much of the fear will vanish. And the best way to get a firm grip on the process is to sit down and work out your game plan. It's a battlefield out there in the home-buying market. Brokers, lawyers and sellers each have their own agendas. Don't think for a moment that their interests and yours necessarily coincide—they don't. They only earn money when you buy and aren't really concerned about your needs and wants. In addition, all real estate transactions take place in private—in a home, an office, a restaurant or a car. Because of this, reliable information about value, price and market trends is difficult to obtain, and, when it is available, costs a fortune.

Real estate businesses hire specialists to stay on top of this underground data. The only sources you have for such information are those very professionals who are indifferent to your needs and wants. That's where I come in. This book is your only true ally in the home buying process. Bring it with you on the buying adventure. Carry it as you would a shield and a sword. It will ensure that you approach the process as an expert, not someone to be taken lightly. It will also help you to devise your game plan—a clear set of goals and the strategy you'll employ to achieve them. This game plan is essential, because without it you can very easily lose sight of your goals, as brokers, lawyers, sellers and the marketplace push you one way and then another.

The process of buying a home is really not as mysterious as the experts have made it seem, yet is *is* the most stressful situation you will ever be involved in. When compared to the hunt for a home, a divorce seems like a day off for the nervous system. Passions rise when home ownership is involved. Potential buyers may fall in love with a home and enter a competitive battle, offering far more than they originally planned, more than the home is actually worth. Every decision is magnified in importance; after all, this is the single biggest purchase in your life, and your future, your hopes, dreams and aspirations, are all wrapped up in those four walls. Logic and business acumen often get lost in the heat of the real estate negotiation. I have watched hardened Wall Streeters rashly double their offers on homes for which they are competing.

I once represented a senior vice–president of a major investment banking house who became so emotionally involved in the bidding process that his motivation shifted from wanting to buy to wanting to win.

I've seen people intimidated into making higher offers when their original bid was characterized as "cheap" or "stupid." They boosted their offers in order to appear more intelligent and less stingy.

I've seen people flattered into making higher offers. A college professor friend of mine was told by a broker that the co-op he had chosen was "a perfect fit." The broker told him that his interest in it showed remarkable insight and wisdom. He finally bought it, but at an inflated price.

My goal in writing this book is to sharpen your skills so

you can cut through the home-buying process to make it a gratifying rather than nerve-racking experience. The best way to make that happen is for you to become your own scout, your own appraiser, your own negotiator. After all, who is better suited?

My guidelines are based on practical case histories rather than abstract theories and data. They are derived from more than thirty years of observing and participating in the home-buying process. Over the years I've been to a couple of closings that resembled funerals, but the great majority have been joyful births.

My mother and father just bought a home. He's eighty-one. They signed a thirty-year mortgage because I firmly believe that mortgages are life extenders. I have four children, none of whom are married yet, but who are all home owners—and they all bought before they could *afford* to. Each has found that through home ownership, their self-confidence has soared, and this has paid rich dividends in many other parts of their lives. Personally, I have owned every kind of home, from a single-family suburban house, to an urban co-op, to a summer home.

You are *going* to buy the best home possible because I am going to equip you with the expertise you need to do just that. Step by step I will walk you through the process of buying a home.

First, we will size up the alternatives out there, decide whether to buy or to build, and examine all the available options—co-ops, condos, single family homes, multiple-family dwellings and attached houses.

We will determine exactly how much buying power you have by looking at your needs, what you can afford, your tax situation and your goals. We will draw up a game plan that maps the best route to your final destination.

An old maxim says that the three keys to real estate are location, location and location. We will conduct a search for an area and show you how to evaluate it.

Next we will assemble the team—broker, lawyer, contractor, accountant, inspector and insurance broker—and find out what the fees are and how and when to pay them. And we'll make sure that all your team members serve you, not just the deal itself.

We'll walk you through the search for *the* house.

You'll become an expert negotiator, privy to the secrets of preparation and expertise, and firm in the knowledge of where all the parties—seller and broker and their intermediaries—are coming from. We'll review the tactics of negotiating, including offers, increments, what to say, and when and where to say it.

We'll prime your inspectors and engineers to examine the property with a fine tooth comb. You'll also learn how to perform your own preliminary inspection. Uncared for property signals its problem to the astute buyer. Certain geographic areas have their own specific problems to look out for, and we will examine these problems and learn how to prepare for them.

The contract is really the most important final step in buying a home. We will examine this document in detail, review what to look for, and what to insist on. At every step of the process we will ensure that you, the buyer, are in control, not left to the mercy of brokers whose only concern is closing the deal, any deal, regardless of how it affects you.

We will choose a bank for a mortgage, run through the interview, and fill out the application together. But, most important, we will prepare for the mortgage application process in advance, examining potential objections and credit difficulties, and straightening them out before they can rear their ugly heads.

For many first-time home buyers, the closing is a mysterious, forbidding event. But through preparation, practice and planning, we will dispel the mists shrouding this cryptic ritual.

The search for new housing is a quest that can be started at any age. Many first time buyers may have parents in the process of buying their last home—a place to retire to. We will discuss the special problems and precautions that older buyers have to take into account and will examine exactly what are the best ways to buy a retirement home.

And finally, we'll help you move—a process that may

seem straightforward, but which can prove treacherous, with its bids that aren't really bids, and its reams of red tape spun out by an uncaring bureaucracy.

Throughout it all we will see how, by taking charge of the process, by becoming your own best expert, and by keeping in mind the traditional values that have compelled you to search for a home in the first place, buying a home can be a joyous and rewarding experience.

CHAPTER TWO

REAL ESTATE: PAST, PRESENT AND FUTURE

*Happy the man whose wish and care
A few paternal acres bound,
Content to breathe his native air
In his own ground.*
ALEXANDER POPE

Home ownership is truly as American as apple pie. Nowhere else in the world is it as economically easy or socially acceptable to own the roof over your head. Indeed, real estate is one of the foundations of our economy, employing millions, not just in the sales, repair and contruction businesses, but in ancillary industries such as building materials, insurance and banking.

And the institution of long-term home mortgages is just as much a part of the fabric of American life—in fact, Americans invented it. When Bill Levitt, of Levittown fame, decided to broaden his holdings and develop middle-income homes across the Atlantic in France he discovered to his chagrin that Frenchmen knew nothing of long-term mortgages. There the norm was a five-year mortgage with a five-year payout. He was forced to abandon the project.

To win the real estate war successfully—and make no mistake, it is a war out there—you have to become an expert, capable of taking control of the process and wending your way through the hazards placed in your path by sellers, developers, builders, brokers and attorneys. And in order to become an expert—to attain the necessary objectivity about the home-buying process—you need to understand the roots of your urge to own a home. In addition, it is useful to understand how and why certain traditions have evolved over the history of real estate in order to understand which traditions you can safely ignore, and which ones suggest valuable rules to follow, even today.

In order to weed out the old wives' tales from the valuable traditions, we need to look at how real estate evolved, from its roots in primitive culture to its contemporary prominence in the modern brain.

There is an almost biological need to own land and to have your own home. We are tied to land, as if by some real estate chromosome. To trace the history of real estate accurately, and to see why we have always been predisposed to own land, we must go all the way back to primitive man.

Primitive man struggled with spear and club to defend his territory from intruders. His "property" rights, though not codified, were fairly complete, certainly more complete than our own today. The earliest known records of real estate transactions are found in the Bible—Jeremiah, for example, bought several hectares from his cousin. Unfortunately, we have no record as to whether he later sold it for a profit.

As populations grew, individuals banded together to help defend their collective land holdings, thus giving up some of those absolute rights they had so assiduously guarded in exchange for a greater degree of security. As the group grew larger, loose centralized authorities were formed. Though the single owner still had possession of property, he often had to relinquish part of his crops or personal property to the central organization. In exchange for this early "property tax," the primitive land owner acquired the right to pass his property on to his heirs.

As the centralized authority gained prominence, it often sought to portray itself as either a supreme deity or an emperor or king whose authority had been granted by God. In Europe, this combination of church and state authority fostered the feudal system, in which royalty handed out leases to allies and relatives, who in turn had serfs and peasants live on and work the land in exchange for a tribute (in either goods or coin) to their lord. The ruler then taxed his underlords for their right to possess the land. Despite, or perhaps because of, constant wars throughout the continent, peasants retained possession of the land, while kings and royalty held ownership and collected rent.

Although the kings of England owned all the land they ruled over, they knew that it was the lowly tenant farmer, growing crops on that land, who made it profitable. The kings therefore let the serfs live on, and off, the land—in fact and practice, possess it—but regularly reaffirmed royal ownership by charging a rent. By implementing this rent system, the kings transcended the traditional idea that possession equaled ownership. The tenant farmer could put a fence around his lot, but the king still owned the fenced-in property. The king might give land away to a loyal knight, but he always retained what was called a "right of reverter"—a clause which stipulated that after a certain length of time, or upon the happening of some event (such as the death of the knight with no heir apparent), the land would revert back to the Crown.

The underlords eventually tired of kicking back a large quantity of their rents to the king. In 1215, the English lords forced King John to sign the Magna Carta, giving the lords greater control over their holdings. Though the king could still tax and draft troops, the state protected the rights of land owners, and even tenants. Laws were passed in the 1400s allowing tenant farmers to fence in their land (in order to keep sheep from straying) and to pass the plot on to their children.

The feudal kings transmitted their edicts on land by messenger, writing down only as much information as was needed. As each edict was passed on, a verbal code of laws developed. This "common law" remains the basis of America's system of real estate laws. Laws which began in an effort to protect the king and his ownership of all he surveyed have evolved into laws that protect your rights to private property. Forty-nine of America's states trace their real estate laws and regulations to English common law. Louisiana, settled by the French, and acquired after the Napoleonic Code had been enacted, is the sole exception.

When I was a banker, I made some loans to developers launching shopping centers in New Orleans. Several mortgages went into default. Accustomed to dealing with the traditions of English common law, I was shocked at the extent to which the Napoleonic Code protected the mortgagors. The developers had three to five years to pay me off and get back their property. Even though I foreclosed, I couldn't touch the property for that period of time—and I still had to pay taxes on it.

Even though common law is applicable in forty-nine of the fifty states, that's still no reason to have just any attorney represent you in the real estate process. While the basis of real estate law is ancient and well-known, the particulars of this complicated business make it essential that the consumer have at his disposal expert professional advice. Customs and the process are different in each state even though they all harken back to common law for their foundation.

When America was settled, land was granted to holding companies by the king of England. These holding companies paid tribute to the Crown, and also passed profits on to the shareholders. With English common law in effect in the colonies, the stage was set for the American Revolution.

The founding fathers, and particularly Thomas Jefferson, were deeply influenced by the philosopher John Locke, who believed that the ownership of property was the ultimate expression of individual freedom and independence. Jefferson took that a step further, believing that the independent farmer, the owner of his own land, would become the backbone of the fledgling republic.

The Jeffersonian ideal underlies the decision to make mortgage interest tax deductible, and helps explain why the United States was the first nation to make thirty-year mortgages acceptable. There has been a conscious effort on the part of the government to encourage home ownership. The GI bill, the secondary mortgage market, the FHA, the Fannie Mae and Ginnie Mae programs have all helped establish home ownership as an important and specially protected part of American life. There is even a cabinet-level post for housing. Even the IRS does its part to encourage home ownership, allowing home sellers to defer taxes on the sale of a home, and even in some instances, exempt them from it completely. During the recent debate over tax reform, no congressman seriously threatened the deductions on home mortgages.

The separation of the thirteen original colonies from the English Crown resulted in ownership of the land passing from the Crown to the colonies themselves, which in turn transferred ownership to the new federal government. Each colony, now a state, retained the common law regulations from the past, retaining the rights to tax, purchase (eminent domain), acquire uninherited land (escheat) and regulate. The states then passed these rights on to cities, towns and villages.

The federal government retained power over lands it deemed vital to interstate commerce—mainly shorelines—and land not owned by the states. These lands were distributed to citizens by sale, or in return for military service. Other lands were handed over to railroad companies as an encouragement to speed up the development of a transportation system. (Though homesteading was abolished in 1976, the federal government still owns one-third of the total land area of the United States.)

Certainly our founding fathers were themselves bitten by the real estate bug. George Washington and Robert Morris (the primary architect of the Constitution and a signer of the Declaration of Independence) both speculated in property around what is now Washington, D.C., but which was then swamps and tidal marshes. Washington evidently had real estate acumen—Mount Vernon certainly has gone up in value. Morris, on the other hand, went broke buying the underwater lots and died in prison.

Into the twentieth century, real estate transactions were governed by the rule of *caveat emptor* (let the buyer beware). But early in the century, the National Association of Real Estate Brokers and other industry associations were formed, bringing some sense of order to the haphazard market. By 1917, states such as California and Oregon were passing legislation to license real estate sellers in an attempt to clean up shady practices in the industry.

It is a fact that real estate laws differ slightly from state to state (there is no federal real estate law), particularly in the degree to which they grant discretion to nonprofessionals such as brokers. However the basics, the essence of real estate, the things to look out for when buying, are the same—first, that the home satisfy your needs and desires; second, that it be a good investment.

But before you follow in the footsteps of English kings and start on your historic journey to home ownership, let's take a short detour to the dictionary in order to define our terms.

All property is divided into two categories: *real property* and *personal property*. Real property is the ground and anything attached to it, from the core of the earth to the sky. Personal property is everything else. A brick carried in your hand is personal property. Once you attach that brick to earth you own, it becomes real property. Personal property can sometimes take on the trappings of real property. Co-ops, for example, are actually personal property. Technically, ownership of a co-op is ownership of certificates of stock in a corporation that owns real estate, which then leases real property to you in perpetuity. The IRS treats the co-op like real property since, in essence, you have possession and almost all the rights of ownership. (I'll delve more deeply into co-ops in Chapter Three.)

There are also different types of ownership. The highest degree of ownership, and the one almost all home owners achieve, is *fee ownership.* This involves the transfer of real property from person to person, through a deed—a document describing the real property, specifying the owner, and noting to whom ownership is being transferred. Fee ownership can be broken down into various other rights. For instance, a fee owner can lease his property. A lease is the surrendering of one of the most important rights to real estate—the possession and enjoyment of the property to the exclusion of others, including in many cases the property owner. A fee owner has actual ownership of the ground, from the earth's core to the sky.

Yet fee ownership without direct possession of the property makes you no more than a landlord. Possession often brings with it the most vital of rights, depending on how long the term of possession is. Leases can run for centuries. (In Chapter Five, which deals with affordability, we will go into the lease—with an option to buy, and long-term contract alternatives—in greater detail.)

When we say that you own up to the sky, we don't mean that you can actually exercise your right to construct a personal Tower of Babel. Sixty years ago, the common belief was that you owned up to the nearest star. But thanks to a New Jersey health farm, you no longer own the path to Alpha Centauri.

Bernard McFadden's health farm was located near a small airport. McFadden's guests were constantly being bothered by lascivious aviators buzzing low over the unencumbered colonists. McFadden was furious. He applied for, and got, a temporary court injunction stopping planes from flying over his property. The case worked its way up to the Supreme Court less than a century ago, where Justice Cardoza cloaked air rights in a slightly fuller suit of clothes. Cardoza ruled that owners of real property do not own up to the heavens; they own only up to what is reasonable for possession and enjoyment. The planes were allowed to fly over McFadden's health farm, but were forbidden to swoop down for a quick peek. Ever since that decision, real property owners' air rights differ from case to case.

So much for the past. Let's take a brief aerial survey of today's real estate market.

Today, the mortgage business has a whole new place in American culture. Years back, American home owners looked at the mortgage as something to get rid of as soon as possible—a sword of Damocles hanging over their heads. When the mortgage was paid off, family and friends gathered to burn the offending paper as a triumphant ritual. Now, the mortgage is a tool for future financial growth rather than a thorn in the side. Mortgages are something to hang on to, not to get rid of, and second mortgages are being used by savvy home owners to finance their futures.

In the early years of a mortgage, the monthly payment is almost completely devoted to paying off interest—thus, it is deductible. As time goes on, a larger and larger share of the monthly payment goes toward paying the principal, rather than the interest. When the mortgage payment reaches the crossover period—when it consists of more principal than interest—an astute home owner may refinance so that his monthly payment once again becomes primarily interest, and thus tax deductible once again. Clearly, the tradition that views the mortgage as an onerous burden is one we can safely ignore.

The mortgage holder himself, or herself, has undergone a remarkable transformation over the last few decades. In the past, the mortgage holder had a handlebar mustache and carried away the farmer's daughter in the event of a default. Today, the friendly mortgage holder will do almost anything to help you avoid default, since he will make less money selling your home to someone new than he would from you if you fulfill your mortgage.

Mortgage banking has changed from a loan business to a securities business. A bank will write 10,000 mortgages in New York, bundle them into one financial instrument, and sell them to a bank in Ohio for a profit. This is called the secondary mortgage market. The Ohio bank becomes heir to the monthly payments. The New York bank made its profit on origination points and other fees. Both banks then reinvest their profits in more mortgages, keeping the money churning. Businesses other than banks also buy these mortgage securities, getting their hands on this most profitable (and secure) of investments.

When double-digit inflation hit the scene in the late seventies, bankers were shaken; after all, if you're lending money at 9 percent and inflation is running 13 percent, you can't make money. Around this time, one brilliant banker came up with the *adjustable rate mortgage* (ARMs). This not only gave banks a hedge against rampaging inflation, but also served to point the way to even more profit potential—by enticing more borrowers with low interest rates in the early years of their mortgage—thus further stimulating the banks to pursue the mortgage business.

Another factor helping to shape today's market is a wider awareness of the simple fact that the supply of real estate is limited. It can't be manufactured or duplicated. Since not all real estate is usable, and development takes that which is off the market, there is a constantly shrinking supply. Couple this with a growing population, and the continuing increase in real estate values appears inevitable.

This shrinking supply also led to the boom in co-op and condo apartments—two devices to increase the number of owners of one particular piece of property. The move toward higher and higher structures is yet another way to increase the density of ownership on a single piece of real estate.

The new *convertible-rate mortgages* are also stimulating home ownership. They offer the advantage of locking in a low interest rate at the outset of the mortgage, with the potential to later lock into a fixed rate with a fee of approximately $250. This lets you play the mortgage market on your own. While the fixed rate that you may eventually convert into indeed won't be as low as the true current fixed interest rate, it will almost certainly be better than the rate you would have to pay should you renegotiate the loan. This convertibility feature can save many thousands of dollars in fees and mortgage expenses.

Another change in the complexion of the real estate market today is the home-buying population, which encompasses more singles and unrelated groups of people. The percentage of home buyers that are traditional families—in form as well as size—has declined. As a result, today's home buyer has priorities that are somewhat different from those of his or her parents and grandparents.

Quality ranks higher than ever before for today's buyer—in both craftsmanship and materials. People shopping for homes now prize amenities as never before. Two-car garages, fireplaces, and central air conditioning are important, often more important than the size of the house itself. Energy efficiency, though not as high a priority as it was during the seventies, remains a consideration. The house of preference for the new home buyer is still the single-family detached house, but not by as large a margin as in the past—co-ops and condo apartments have become acceptable to more and more buyers.

Pre-war apartment buildings (those built prior to 1945) are increasingly more attractive to buyers. They have a never diminishing value and character that the newer ''cookie-cutter'' apartments lack.

The average buyer today looks for a home with a separate master bedroom suite, a two-car garage, two and one-half bathrooms, a full basement, an informal eating area instead of a dining room, walk-in closets, bay windows, and French doors.

Buyers still favor the suburbs more than the inner cities, though they look for a suburban location that lets them travel to work in a shorter time.

Another important trend in today's market is the rehabilitation of existing homes. With construction costs skyrocketing, and demand for quality space still high, buyers search out older, somewhat dilapidated homes, and reconstruct or restore them to meet their dreams and expectations. Homes built before World War II—the antique home market—are hot commodities today.

Because of the shortage of affordable urban homes, commercial space is frequently being converted to residential use today. New York City artists pioneered this process, by searching out abandoned warehouse lofts with lots of open, bright space in run-down industrial neighborhoods, and converting them—legally and illegally—into modern residences.

Despite all these new twists in buyer tastes and preferences, the real estate market has always been defined by two well-known phrases: *seller's market* and *buyer's market*. A seller's market is one in which the advantage is skewed in favor of the current owner of the property. For example, in a seller's market a home might go on the market for $200,000 and receive an immediate offer at that level. The seller might then remove the home from the market and raise his price. A buyer's market is one in which there is a glut of available homes for buyers to choose from, driving prices down, and drawing out the time it takes to sell.

In the United States right now there are examples of both buyer's and seller's markets. The California coast—comprising the San Francisco, San Diego and Los Angeles markets—is as hot a seller's market as we are apt to see for many years. The market verges on insanity right now, with emotions running high and idiocy prevailing. While there are some other pockets of seller's markets in America, most of the rest of the country is made up of buyer's markets because of the depressed industrial economy and the consequent loss of jobs. (For a detailed examination of market trends in the nation's geographic areas, see Appendix E.)

In general, home ownership is more popular than ever today. Mortgage rates are once again within reason, luring more and more Americans into the market. The urge to buy can perhaps best be illustrated by the fact that Americans who bought homes when the mortgage rates were astronomical, are choosing to buy new, more expensive homes, rather than use the falling rates to reduce their indebtedness.

It's always difficult to predict future trends in the real estate market. Construction is generally planned three to four years in advance, and always seems too great or too little to suit today's buying trends. Because of this time lag, real estate in turn often lags behind the economy. Now that I've made a convenient escape hatch for myself, I'll stick my neck out and paint a picture of tomorrow's American real estate market.

The most useful statistical source for any real estate prognosticator is population demographics; and these demographics indicate that housing will undergo some remarkable changes in the future. The baby boomers (those born between 1946 and 1960) are getting older. They have already bought their first homes and established families, and are about to enter middle age. Close on their heels is the baby bust generation (born after 1961), now reaching home-buying age. These baby busters are a different breed. They are marrying even later than their predecessors, and therefore starting families later. However, they are not delaying their purchase of shelter. These young unmarried people are becoming the hottest home buying group. Accordingly, multifamily dwellings, offering a greater amount of smaller homes on a given piece of land, are soaring in popularity, and will become the primary first home.

Meanwhile, the baby boomers will find their wallets brimming with extra cash as they reach their prime income-earning age. These affluent baby boomers will find themselves house-poor, and will begin to search for step-up homes—larger, more luxurious places to accommodate their growing families. Look for high-end, expensive houses to be the hot single-family buy of the future. And watch for the continuing, even increasing, importance of and demand for co-op and condo apartments due to the ever shrinking availability of land for single-family home development.

But even as these trends take their place, there is another demographic group looming large for any seers: the baby boom echo—the children of baby boomers. Currently bouncing on yuppie knees, the baby boom echo can be expected to revitalize the affordable single family home market as we enter the twenty-first century.

With that said, there are certain truths that will remain constant whatever the current or future trends: people will always want homes—perhaps in new configurations or in new areas—and the purchase will always be stressful. The single best way to overcome this anxiety is the subject of my next chapter, which is all about setting realistic goals for yourself.

CHAPTER THREE

THE GAME PLAN: SETTING GOALS AND APPRAISING YOUR NEEDS

A map of the world that does not include Utopia is not even worth glancing at.
OSCAR WILDE

To navigate successfully the minefields others will place in your path, it is essential that you know exactly where you want to be going, and what you want to achieve. Buying a home is a highly stressful process, and you want to be prepared for it. If you know your needs and wants, and keep to your buying plan, you will take some of the power away from the seller and be better able to control the situation. The real estate market is more complicated than the New York Giants' defense, and you'll need a sophisticated, all encompassing game plan if you're going to come out on top. This game plan is just as important as a business plan is to a fledgling entrepreneur—it gives you focus and prevents you from becoming sidetracked.

The home that you buy must meet two very different types of criteria. First, it must be space that you love. Second, it must be a good investment. In this chapter I will help you to develop a series of goals—your needs and wants in a living space—to determine what wonderful space means to you. In Chapter Six I'll show you how to make sure your investment is sound. For now, let's concentrate on finding out exactly what your dream home looks like. We'll do that by reviewing some of the basic components of homes and by finding out exactly how important each is to you.

The first step in putting your dream on paper is to examine your current home. Take out piece of paper and write down everything you like about it. Include all the physical aspects of your present home but don't overlook the emotional and social ones. If you like being within walking distance of a museum, write that down. If you've enjoyed being far from your neighbors, make a note of it. Though this exercise may make you momentarily rethink a change of venue, the next step will reinforce your desire to buy a new home.

On another sheet of paper, write down everything you don't like about your current home. Is it too noisy? Write that down. Too far from work? Make a note. Now, take a third piece of paper and combine the two lists in adjacent columns. What you have in front of you is more than just a set of likes and dislikes—it's the first part of your game plan for buying a home. Based on this little bit of self-analysis, you can make some major decisions on what type of home would best suit you and what type of location you would be happiest living in.

Once you have combined the lists, categorize each item as being very important, marginally important, or only slightly important. Rewrite the list, placing the most important items near the top, the least important at the bottom. This is no time for rationalizing or second-guessing your feelings. Be searching, fearless, and brutally honest. Don't say you like being close to museums just because it sounds good. How important could it be if you haven't been inside one in the past five years?

To ensure that you touch all the bases and establish as complete a game plan as possible, you will have to analyze your feelings and priorities on a whole series of home attributes and variables. Ask yourself questions that will help you get in touch with what you value. While it's not up to me to set priorities for you, there are five primary aspects of any home—single family or multifamily, attached or detached, new or old—that are the most important to examine. It's up to you to determine their relative importance to you.

PROXIMITY TO WORK

Most of your day is going to be spent at work, not at home. How much time are you willing to spend traveling to and from work? In general, the farther from your workplace you live (assuming you work in or near the urban core), the more house you will get for your money. You must decide: Are you willing to rearrange your work and leisure habits to accommodate a longer traveling schedule? Will you be able to do work on the train? Can you do dictation in the car?

And remember, it isn't just the trip to work itself that takes time. It takes time to get to the train, for example, and in winter or inclement weather a one-hour train ride can in fact take several hours. Don't assume that printed schedules are always followed.

Commuting time isn't always a drawback. When I began teaching finance at C.W. Post College on Long Island, I took advantage of the commute—I put a tape deck in my car, bought some tapes, and proceeded to learn a foreign language.

Distance is one of the biggest games being played in real estate today. The words *next* and *near* no longer have any real meaning. These terms may satisfy the state laws governing truth in advertising, but they may have no basis in the real world. What legally qualifies as being "near" a railroad station may still require a twenty-minute car ride. The only way to check distance is to walk or drive it yourself.

When I lived in Woodbury, a town on Long Island, I learned this the hard way. I took a job as president of a company headquartered in Manhattan. One of the conditions of the job was that the company would help bridge the distance between my home and the office by providing me with a car and driver. While the car was comfortable, being picked up at 5:30 in the morning and deposited home at 8:00 at night didn't make the distance any more tolerable.

PRICE

(For a complete analysis of what you can afford to spend on a home see Chapter Five.)

PRIVACY

Do you enjoy having neighbors nearby? Is it important to you to be part of a community? Would you prefer not to see, as well as not to talk to, anyone outside your home? As I will demonstrate in the next chapter, your desire for privacy will determine not only the type of home you buy, and where you buy it, but whether that home is new or old as well.

Everyone dreams of owning his or her own castle, but that doesn't mean everyone can actually live in and enjoy bucolic seclusion. Some of us can't live without some noise and activity—Woody Allen isn't the only one who can't stand the great outdoors. For my own part, I could never understand what people see in lawns and landscaping. To me they are just drains on the wallet and ways to waste weekends.

SPACE

How large a home do you need and want? To figure out what size home you need, take a look at the size of your family and its living patterns. A home should have as many rooms as you need. Make a conscious effort to visualize, and think in, square footage, rather than just the number of rooms.

I never knew how much convenience an extra bathroom could add to my life. When one of my daughters left home I inherited her bathroom. Before that I had shared a bathroom with my wife. Not having to wait to use the bathroom and feeling free to luxuriate as long as you want in a hot bath are two of the joys of owning a home.

Do you need a few large rooms, or more smaller rooms? Rooms to entertain in are great, but how often are you really going to use them? Look at your home as a combination of shared and private spaces. Do you all watch television together, or separately? Do you need that large family room, or would it be better to have TVs in each bedroom? How often are you going to use a bedroom sitting area? Sure, a formal dining room can be a wonderful thing. But does your family dine formally? Sometimes it's better to have a larger, more comfortable kitchen, especially if you belong to the great American tradition of kitchen sitters. I think there is a genetic predisposition toward doing things in the kitchen. Make sure that there is at least some place to eat. If a home you are looking at doesn't have either a dining room or an eat-in kitchen, it's too small to buy.

A good rule of thumb is to figure out the number of rooms you need, and then add one. The reason is that adding rooms, whether by building up or converting a basement or garage, is more expensive than buying a house that has an added room. It's also possible that adding on a room could destroy the architecture of your new house. It is better to buy a home with more, smaller rooms, than one with fewer, larger rooms since the former provides more privacy—one of the major reasons for buying a home in the first place.

LIGHT AND VIEW

Despite all the magic tricks that architects, designers, and decorators have up their sleeves, there are no substitutes for light and views. Windows which offer dazzling light and pleasing views can make an otherwise mediocre home extraordinary. How many windows do you want? Are you willing to sacrifice light for privacy? Fresh air is especially important to consider when you are buying an apartment. Windows overlooking a backyard or alleyway will probably offer little light and no relief in the summer heat.

Once you have answered all the questions about these five most important aspects of a home, begin considering all the other criteria that go into choosing a home.

PROXIMITY TO SHOPPING How important is shopping to you? Is it something you do out of necessity, or is shopping an important part of your recreation? Do you like walking to stores, or do you prefer to drive? Certainly you need to be near a supermarket, a dry cleaner, and a drugstore (not to mention a deli and a Chinese take-out restaurant), but do you also need to be close to boutiques and record stores?

WORKMANSHIP One of the joys of an older home, or one that is custom-built for you, is the degree of craftsmanship that went into its construction. Superior workmanship can be very important when it comes time to sell your home, but it can also be a trap. I have a library at home that is lined with hand-carved, hand-painted paneling. There are even wood knots painted on the plaster. The room could be put to much better use, but there's nothing I can do with it, except preserve it. I'm a captive of the room's superior workmanship.

PROXIMITY TO SCHOOLS Are good, local schools important to you and your family *now*? Or will it be several years before they'll matter? You'll pay a premium to live in a superior school district, and you may be giving up other things that are important to you today. Buy for schools only when it's necessary, and make sure you are buying reality, not just reputation. Are you willing to pay the higher taxes and higher home prices that go along with the better school districts? Don't buy schools for the future—they could well decline in quality before your family has the chance to make use of them.

One of the reasons my wife and I bought our co-op in New York City was because it was located in what was considered a superior school district. My wife sat in on a class after we had closed on the co-op, and was shocked at how bad it was. We ended up sending our children to private school, and still paid a premium for the public school district. In effect, we paid twice for our children's schooling.

ENERGY EFFICIENCY Do you have a crystal ball that tells you what the energy situation will be in five years? If you do, perhaps you should go into the stock market instead of buying real estate. Don't buy energy efficiency just because it sounds good. If the current situation—or your area's climate—dictates placing a priority on energy efficiency, fine. Watch out for unproven new types of energy that have no history behind them but merely the manufacturer's test reports. The best way to achieve energy efficiency is to turn the thermostat down.

EXTERIOR APPEARANCE Since the outside of your home is the first thing you and others see, obviously it is important. Usually, the most important consideration is that the exterior of your home should be in keeping with the neighborhood's character. Too idiosyncratic an exterior can hurt you when it comes time to sell.

OUTDOOR AREAS Do you like to grow things? Is it important for you to be able to spend time outdoors? Remember that landscaping and grounds are very costly to maintain. Is the high maintenance factor justified by your desire and need for landscaping? Outdoor living areas, such as decks, which are not as costly to maintain, can add immeasurably to your enjoyment of a home. In addition, they improve the home's marketability. Ask yourself: Will you actually use outdoor facilities? Beautiful landscaping and sweeping lawns are wonderful, but if all you are going to use them for are a wedding or two, you might want to rethink their importance.

The importance of outdoor areas depends on your own personal habits, likes, and dislikes. My son has inherited his grandfather's love of planting and growing things in the earth. I, on the other hand, look at yard work as a sentence on Devil's Island.

BASEMENTS Do you really have use for a basement? Many people only come up with uses for a basement when they are forced to. There is no hard and fast rule that says a home needs a basement. And don't plan on increasing the value of your home by finishing the basement. Adding rooms below ground level doesn't add value to a home. Crawl spaces can often perform all the structural functions of a basement, insulation, space for plumbing and electrical conduits.

HEATING AND COOLING Is your home situated in a region where, because of extreme temperatures, you will need extraordinary heating or cooling systems? How sensitive are you to heat and cold? Are you willing to wear a sweater around the house? Is central air conditioning a necessity?

CLOSETS Are you a clothing collector? Do you or members of your family need unusual amounts of storage? Have at least one closet for every member of the family, and then add two.

GARAGES Do you treat your car like a member of the family? Then, by all means, provide it with its own room. Otherwise garages aren't worth the extra cost.

After you have answered all these questions, and any others you can think of (these are only suggested questions, meant to act as a guide), decide which of these goals you might be willing to give up, and which you wouldn't. It's important to make these decisions now, before you have begun looking at houses. Tabulate your answers to these questions, and classify them as essential, desirable or a dream: something you'd like but can easily live without. Place the essentials at the top of your final game plan, followed by the desirables and lastly the dreams. This final checklist will be your conscience during the remainder of the home-buying adventure. It will help keep you from falling in love with a house and letting infatuation get the better of you. If you keep your game plan handy you can refer to it regularly, keeping your goals in the forefront of your mind, and not letting that magnificent pink elephant steal your heart. Remember: Don't fall in love with a home until you own it.

There's a lot of noise and big buck fever out there in the real estate market. Brokers and sellers will tempt you with extravagant claims. Magazines will preach to you about the latest trends in home design. These goals will help you filter out the static and streamline the process, giving you a clear picture of the home you need and want.

You're also going to have to keep a clear head because of the tricks that savvy sellers will play with you. They'll put a stick of cinnamon in the oven so the home smells cozy. They will empty their closets to make them look bigger. Rooms will be sparsely furnished to exaggerate their size. Water damage in a sly seller's home may be hidden by a fresh coat of paint. Mirrors may be used to turn a tiny space into an extra room. I've even seen sellers touch up their chipped appliances with Liquid Paper. Remember that when you look at a home it will be at its best—light brighter than ever (thanks to increased bulb wattage), windows sparkling clean, shades and drapes wide open. Sellers may invest as much as $5,000 in camouflage to disguise, or just distract you from, the home's problems.

But thanks to your game plan, you're going to look at everything objectively. You'll have a tape measure with you. (And you'll make sure to hold the smart end—the one that gives you the measurement.) You'll take some photos. And above all, you'll bear in mind your goals. I'm not going to let a wily broker convince you that a home is perfect for you when it really isn't.

You've got to keep your head in the buying process, and sometimes nothing is more difficult. The purchase of a home involves a transformation in your lifestyle and habits. It involves your heart, dreams, ego, genes and upbringing. A solid game plan, with your needs, wants and goals clearly spelled out, will keep your mind involved as well.

CHAPTER FOUR

THE
ALTERNATIVES

The old order changeth,
yielding place to new.
ALFRED, LORD TENNYSON

With your housing goals written down on a fresh legal pad, and etched into your gray matter, it's time to make the first concrete decisions about your future home. While the traditional image of an American home is a single-family detached house on a quarter-acre plot with a white picket fence around the perimeter, today's complex real estate market has spawned a wide variety of home options, from the pre-war cooperative apartment in the city to the brand new home in a resort association.

Before you start worrying about the type of home that best suits your goals, you'll have to choose between a newly built house and an old home. Each has its advantages and disadvantages, and only by carefully assessing your own needs and wants once again, can you make this first, and perhaps most difficult choice.

Many times, the first instinct of a potential home buyer is to look for a new home, one that hasn't been sullied by a series of varied residents. Often people feel they must settle for an old home, since newer homes with the same characteristics have traditionally cost many times more than old ones.

While old homes may have seen their share of abuse, they are just as likely to have received tender loving care for a long peiod of time. Today we see a renewed interest in traditional styles of architecture and design, and the growing popularity of "antique" houses. This has narrowed the price difference between old and new homes. Many people are discovering that older homes have a distinct personality, with details and craftsmanship that newer homes can't match. But along with that increased character come greater maintenance demands.

It's easier to buy a new home—more is disclosed and evident to the naked eye. Construction details can be observed in a new home, and you will have a better shot at making an accurate evaluation of the structure's soundness. New homes haven't been buffeted by the elements for years and years, and you are protected by the latest regulations of the local building department and the state's construction codes. You'll have a clearer map of the home itself—you can examine the blueprint—and can at least be sure there is no asbestos lurking in the walls.

If the home is brand-new, and has been built by a reputable builder, it might be possible to bypass hiring an engineer for an inspection, but I don't recommend it. The inspection will certainly be easier, since the inspector needn't worry about finding problems associated with age, such as dry rot. However, factors such as water sources may become more important—if well water is to be used, for example, you'll have to have the inspector find out if the well is deep enough. In some states, new homes carry a guarantee, often with the imprint of the state legislature upon it.

With new homes you can avoid inheriting those owners' do-it-yourself projects that often do not measure up to the building code. With insurance companies itching for a reason to deny claims, it is vital that additions and alterations be up to code.

While new homes reveal a great deal more about their structures, their newness tends to leave the future character of their neighborhood shrouded in mystery. Older homes are usually found in areas with established personalities, for better or worse. You risk a great deal more when you buy into a neighborhood that hasn't been established—who knows how it will develop? When I bought my first home—a tract house in a suburban development—all my wife and I saw were the beautiful fields around it. It was only after we had lived there for a year or two that we realized just how many houses the town had allowed the developers to shoehorn into those fields. We also found that in our new town it was more important that the volunteer firemen have brand new uniforms than that the town have a public library. When we first looked at the house, I spotted railroad tracks near our lot, and asked the broker about them. She assured me that this was only a spur line, and plans were in the works to eliminate it entirely. She probably wasn't lying. She just failed to tell me that this was the only spur line in America that had trains running on it every twenty minutes. And as far as I know, plans are still in the works to close it down . . . thirty years later.

Our next home was in another newly developed area—this one with a library. We were moving up to a better, more affluent neighborhood. Being a new area, the values of the community were still being formed.

One day I received a phone call from a neighbor. He told me that he had seen a white Lincoln driving around the area looking at homes. It was driven by a black man. My neighbor said that we had better do something about it. My answer was "Yes, we ought to welcome them." Mine turned out to be the minority opinion. The community split into two warring camps. Neighbors told their children not to play with my kids. My wife and I were ostracized for years afterwards.

This was my first exposure to the then-popular view which held that a black family in a community would reduce property values 50 percent. The black man—who turned out to be a doctor—moved in. But by that time my family and I had soured on the area; the silent treatment can do that to you. I sold my home for $78,000. What happened to property values? Today, homes there sell for between $300,000 and $750,000. So much for declining values. This nouveau riche community was simply not sophisticated enough to deal with changing social values.

The heating and electrical costs of older homes are more predictable than those of a new home. You will have the entire history of a home's bills to forecast future costs. With a new home, you can only guess what the costs will be. One thing is going for you with a new home, however: It will have the latest in insulation and climate control technology.

The process of purchasing new and old homes can differ drastically. Many new homes are bought unbuilt, from a model—a model situated perfectly, flooded with natural light and possessing a stupendous view. It will also be professionally decorated to accentuate the positive and disguise the negative. The view from your unit may take in the nearby parking lot, rather than that magnificent lake. And that beautiful group of trees which looks so good from the model's picture window could be the same one blocking all the sunlight from your living room.

If you are buying from a blueprint, the odds are actually more in the seller's favor. The appearance of a house changes as the earth revolves. A home on a piece of paper doesn't tell you what the light is like at sunrise, or how the winds blow against the front door in January. Also, new homes are often bought from a developer, or his agent—players who aren't likely to negotiate price.

(The sale of a new home has become a mechanical process in the larger urban areas. In fact, some sellers will tell you that a lawyer isn't needed. Don't believe them. That's like the wolf telling the three little pigs that they can leave the front door wide open. The only time buying from a blueprint may pay off is in the purchase of a high-rise apartment. Often, while a new cooperative or condominium building is going up, the developer may try to stimulate sales and raise cash by offering the units at a low price. The developer may not be sure of prices and could be testing the market.

In general, old homes leave more room for creative negotiating. But beware, because savvy sellers of older homes can be sneakier than the most money-conscious developer. They will do their best to cover up any of the house's problems.

Besides the physical and procedural distinctions between buying old and new homes, the emotional character of the purchase is different. When you move into a new home you are surrounded by other new homeowners. There is a shared sense of adventure that brings you together and out of which friendships spring. In new neighborhoods there is less fear—someone is probably looking out for your children, your dog and your car; you'll never have to search for someone to help shovel the snow.

In established neighborhoods, the pattern of everybody's lives is already well-established. It could take ten years before you'd be invited to a cocktail party or card game. But at least you'll be aware of the community's values. In new neighborhoods, a community's values might not evolve along lines with which you are comfortable.

When my family moved from the suburbs into our current home, a pre-war cooperative apartment in New York City, we were stunned to find that our new neighbors didn't so much as say hello, even when we met in the confines of an 8 × 8–foot elevator. I thought that the elevator ride up to my eleventh floor apartment would be a social event. Instead, all eyes focus on the ceiling and no words are exchanged. The most we get is a terse nod of acknowledgment.

Thirty-three years ago my family and I began renting a summer home on Martha's Vineyard. After three years as a part-time resident, we bought land and built our own home. I thought that once we had built a home we would be considered insiders. Far from it. Thirty years later the residents still consider us outsiders.

The choice between a new home and an old home really depends on your personality. Each is an adventure in its own right. Keep this in mind: a new neighborhood, with an indistinct, undetermined character, can develop into an established, upscale community—and an established one can sometimes degenerate.

There is still one more decision to make before you choose the type of home you are going to buy: the form of home ownership that best suits your needs and wants. There are four different ways to own your own home, each with its own pluses and minuses.

The most common form of ownership is *fee simple,* in which you own the buildng and the land it stands on, from one property line to the other. You have complete rights to possess and use the land to the exclusion of others. This type of ownership is traditionally found in single-family detached homes, but can also be applied to the units in single-family attached homes, such as townhouses, brownstones, and rowhouses. Fee simple offers the most private and secure form of ownership—you have control over your property, as well as the structure, and no one else has any rights to it. However, because of these extensive rights, it is the most expensive form of ownership. Since it is also the most common, fee simple is familiar to most builders, attorneys, inspectors and brokers, and therefore will present the fewest complications when dealing with these professionals.

An increasingly popular form of ownership is the *condominium* in which you fully own your home, and jointly own common facilities—such as lawns, gardens, walkways, hallways, stairs, laundry room and elevators—with your neighbors. Your share of this communal property is as much a part of your ownership deed as the ceiling and floor of your home. Condominiums are generally multifamily attached dwellings, but can also be single-family homes in a development. Condos are cheaper than fee simple homes, since the piece of property accommodates many more living units and the costs of some areas are shared. Another advantage of the condo is that the owner often has more facilities and amenities at his disposal than the fee simple owner. But the flip side is that condos generally don't appreciate as rapidly as fee simple homes. In addition, the owner must pay a common area charge to cover the upkeep of the common property, as well as applicable taxes. That makes every owner a landlord, and owners must decide together when to reduce fees and let needed repairs go, or institute higher maintenance fees to allow for emergency repairs. Condos offer all the tax advantages of the fee simple home and give you freedom to sell to anyone you choose. You also retain a certain degree of autonomy—unlike a co-op, you don't have a problem if your neighbors default on their mortgage; their unit would be the only part of the condo to be foreclosed. There are substantial legal differences between the purchase of a fee simple home and a condominium. If you are thinking of buying a condo, then you, your attorney or your accountant must investigate the bylaws and the declaration of the development for your rights to do construction, reconstruction and any approvals that might be required to sell. Most condos have written into their bylaws a **right of first refusal**, which means that the home must first be offered to the board of managers. Every condo board requires that you pass to them power of attorney to represent you as to the common areas. In addition, the purchase of a condo, or a co-op, which I will discuss with you in the next section, entails legal entanglements that must be examined by a skilled, experienced attorney.

One of the newer forms of home ownership is the **cooperative** (or **co-op**). In a co-op, you own shares in a corporation which in turn owns the building. In legal terms; you don't actually own real estate, but instead personal property—stock in the corporation. However, the IRS treats the co-op as real estate. Co-ops are most often multifamily dwellings; some of the finest, most luxurious apartment houses in America are co-ops. Many co-op buildings have balloon mortgages which could require owners to make a large final payment when the note comes due. More often, another mortgage is taken—

sometimes at a much higher rate—thus increasing the individual co-op owners' costs dramatically. The existence of this underlying mortgage makes it imperative that co-op buyers hire an additional expert, usually an accountant, to check into the building's financial status.

Traditionally, co-ops are cheaper than condominiums, since your purchase price covers only the difference between the corporation's mortgage on the building and its fair market value. (Thus the purchase of a co-op gives you another layer of leverage represented by your share of the underlying mortgage.) Generally you will get more square footage for your dollar when buying a co-op as opposed to a condo, thanks to this underlying mortgage. While this lower initial cost is an advantage, it is offset by higher maintenance costs, since these include the co-op corporation's mortgage payments as well as the upkeep on the building. Monthly payments for a co-op increase faster than those for a condo, since the payments include the costs of fuel oil, labor, insurance, interest and other charges which are subject to inflation and cost of living increases.

When deciding whether or not you can afford a co-op you will have to factor together both the monthly mortgage payment and the maintenance. In fact, the inspection of the co-op's financial status is just as important as the the inspection of the apartment and building's physical systems. The evaluation of a co-op combines the purchase price and the maintenance. Today's rule of thumb is that every hundred dollars of maintenance should be considered another $10,000 added to the purchase price. There are many sick co-ops on the market today whose problems, in the past, have been covered up by inflation. They are now visibly ailing, however, since their underlying mortgages are coming due. Therefore, shopping for the co-op should never be a do-it-yourself process. It is complicated, but a team of skilled, experienced professionals can make the process manageable. The purchase of a co-op is akin to the purchase of stock in a closed corporation; while it's complex and possibly risky, it nevertheless offers the potential for tremendous personal and financial benefits.

The biggest disadvantage to co-ops, however, is the degree to which you are tied, financially and socially, to your neighbors. Co-ops are managed by a board comprised of residents. As a rule of thumb, boards are initially made up of caring, responsible activists. But as time goes on, the snobs and the fanatics often take over a board and turn it into a quasi-fascist organization. A good board can make a building a wonderful place to live. A bad board can make the co-op an obnoxious, snooty trap that first keeps you from buying and then won't allow you to sell to whomever you choose. Buyers must be approved by the board, and often their decisions are based on religion, race, social class, occupation—any issue in fact, on which they choose to discriminate.

Two of my daughters were turned down by co-op boards, I believe, because of their sex, combined with the fact that they were single and self-employed. In both cases I had to enter the scene and personally guarantee their maintenance payments. Since co-op owners are responsible when a member defaults, boards check the financial background of potential buyers; they often require that you have a net worth three times that of the price of the home, and/or pay for the home in cash. Or they may specify the allowable financing and down payments they deem acceptable.

These discriminating ownership criteria are actually attractive to many buyers. There's a story told in New York about a man who had plastic surgery and changed his religion in order to be accepted by a particular building's board.

Soon after I moved into my co-op, I was visited by the super and two members of the board. I thought they were just being good neighbors. I took them on a tour of the apartment and offered them coffee. It turned out they had come to complain that my daughter's game of jacks, played on a wooden floor, was disturbing the downstairs neighbor. They reminded me that a stipulation in the co-op's bylaws required that 90 percent of the apartment had to be carpeted. Worried that they could somehow rescind my co-op membership, I foolishly acceded to the implied threat and carpeted the apartment—something we hadn't wanted to do. The co-op board's evaluation of you is second in importance only to your evaluation of the co-op board before you buy. In general, co-ops are as good or as bad as their board. After thirty years of experience in real estate, I have seen two identical co-ops differ by as much as 50 percent in price, due to the fact that one was well managed and one was not.

Savvy local real estate brokers are excellent sources on the character of a board. By studying the balance sheet and footnotes for a period of years, a skillful real estate attorney can make an estimate of the board's professionalism through their approach to management problems. The super and the managing agent can give you an earful if they are willing to talk.

A less common form of ownership is an **association**, in which you fully own your home and the land it stands on, and also share ownership of a communal recreation area with your neighbors. Generally, associations involve single-family detached homes in a vacation or recreation area—often by a lake or beach. These common holdings are the main advantage of association ownership, since they will be more convenient and private than comparable public facilities. Membership fees are usually charged, but these will be less than those in private clubs. The disadvantage of association ownership is that you give up a great deal of privacy, and are forced to pay fees for the common area, whether you use it or not. Some associations stipulate that any construction you do must conform to their own architectural guidelines. Your aesthetic vision had better fall into line with their dream world, otherwise forget it. Associations differ from condominiums in that they are generally single-family homes on individual lots in a subdivision, as opposed to townhouses or apartments. In addition, association members pay a separate fee for any common recreational facility, rather than having the common charges included in the monthly maintenance fee as they are in a condominium.

The rarest form of ownership is the **partnership**, in which two or more individuals share the down payment, maintenance and mortgage payment costs. Partnership ownership has become popular in large, older houses that can be split into two substantial homes. Many singles today are finding that a partnership arrangement can be their ticket to home ownership. What is essential in this kind of arrangement is compatibility. Partners should know almost everything about one another, including their financial situations. In an arrangement this complicated, with provisions needed for the division of amenities, rights and responsibilities, as well as expenses, it is vital that an experienced attorney draw up the agreement.

In the past few years I have represented many single men and women who have bought homes as part of a partnership. The major stumbling block in the agreement is determining what happens when the relationship has problems and one partner chooses to move out or sell. A home-owning partnership is an ideal arrangement for young unmarried people, but it requires extreme candor before you close the deal.

While there are several types of home ownership to choose from, there is an even greater variety when it comes to selecting a type of home.

The most popular and sought after home in America is the **detached house**, which sits on its own lot. The detached home offers the greatest amount of space and the most privacy. But you won't get this space and privacy for nothing—detached homes are the most expensive type of home to purchase. (Throughout this section, let's assume, for the sake of discussion, that all these types of homes are located in comparable areas. This means that home type, and not location, determines the cost.) And that's to say nothing of the upkeep, heating and cooling costs. Because they are exposed to the elements on all sides, detached homes are the most expensive to heat and cool. The property you buy with your detached home often requires substantial care and expense. Yet, despite the higher costs, the detached house is as close as you're ever going to get to stepping into the regal shoes of those English kings who started the real estate business.

Attached houses, whether single family (townhouses, rowhouses or brownstones), two family or quadruplexes (four family), offer many of the advantages of detached homes, while sacrificing some of the privacy. Attached houses require you to share a common wall or to have one or two walls flush against those of neighbors. Outdoor spaces are often smaller than those of detached homes. Because of these compromises, attached homes generally cost less than detached homes, both to purchase and to maintain. Heating and cooling costs are also lower, since the adjacent homes provide added insulation. If you are comfortable with a more urban lifestyle, an attached home may be right for you. Just remember that the "party wall" means your life will be more closely intertwined with your neighbor's.

Multifamily homes (two- or three-family houses) are not the most attractive houses architecturally. They are often boxy and don't offer the privacy—indoors or out—that detached, or even attached homes provide. And they generally cost more as well. The reason for this discrepancy is that a multifamily home offers an investment opportunity for a single owner. Renting a unit or two can help pay the mortgage and cover maintenance. In addition, rental properties offer depreciation and various other deductions on your tax return. When more than one owner is involved, multifamily homes can help individuals who are unable to afford a home of their own. They can now take advantage of ownership by taking on partners. Multifamily homes offer almost as much autonomy to the owner as detached or attached single-family homes and clearly more than the co-op or condo, since he is free to make any changes or alterations he desires. He can also sell or rent to whomever he pleases.

Apartments are the most inexpensive type of home to buy and maintain. They are found in structures ranging from urban high rises to suburban two-story garden apartments. Co-ops and condo apartments have their own advantages, as we have previously noted. But if you must generalize about apartments, it is safe to assume that they will offer less space and less privacy than any other type of home. They are often more conveniently located, however, and are considerably less expensive to maintain.

A new type of living unit in today's market is the *planned unit development (PUD).* Developers purchase a large tract of land, generally on the fringes of suburbia, and actually create a new town by building everything from high rises, attached houses and detached houses, to stores, offices, recreation facilities, schools and municipal services. Prices in a new PUD are often lower than similar homes in conventional areas. But you may not fit comfortably into the life-style patterns that the developers have laid out. While it may be convenient to work, shop and live in a PUD, if you choose to do anything outside the development you will have given up one of the key advantages of PUD living: proximity. Mission Viejo in California is perhaps the most famous PUD in the country. Its success seems assured. But many other PUDs are not doing as well. Establishing a PUD requires the developer to put a tremendous amount of money into the ground. As development speeds up or slows down, the builder is tempted to trim the amount and quality of the services and recreational facilities, placing a larger burden on schools, stores and services than was originally planned and promised. All that open land suddenly becomes packed with more housing units, instead of recreational facilities. Some observers predict that PUDs are destined to fail because the entrepreneur is trying to play the role of God.

I have owned a co-op, a condo, a detached house and at one time was in a partnership agreement for ownership of a summer home. There are advantages and disadvantages to each style—and each suits different purposes and circumstances.

Now that you have an idea of the various types of homes available to you, take another sheet from your trusty yellow legal pad and see how many of your goals each type can satisfy. Decide upon a form of ownership. And make that difficult choice between an old or a new home. As you've seen, each of these options has its own advantages and disadvantages. The key is to find the one that best suits you—and satisfies as many of the "essentials" and "desirables" on your game plan. It's as if you have a choice between several different jackets, each with the same size written on the label, but each with its own distinctive fit. Some have sleeves that are a tad too long. Others are too tight across the shoulders. But there is bound to be one that fits just right.

CHAPTER FIVE

GETTING DOWN TO DOLLARS: AFFORDABILITY AND DOWN PAYMENTS

*Keep your accounts on your
thumb nail.*
HENRY DAVID THOREAU

Ask almost any American for a formula on home affordability and you'll get a simple, workmanlike answer. He or she will tell you either that 30 percent of your monthly income is the most you can spend on a mortgage payment, or that you can afford a house that costs two or two and a half times your yearly income. They aren't completely wrong. They've just been brainwashed.

Throughout the thirty years I have spent as a financial and real estate consultant, I have found that the primary question clients have about a home, before they ask if it is a good investment, is "Can I afford it?" Housepainters, authors and Wall Street investment bankers are all equally perplexed when it comes time to figuring out their "affordability."

The traditional rules of affordability come from the "other side"—from the bankers who loan mortgage money and the brokers who steer you to available homes. Neither group really cares about your welfare. A banker sits down with your weekly pay stub and multiplies it by four to determine your monthly salary. He then adds to it any other sources of income you receive on a regular basis. Our friendly banker then reaches into his bag of tricks and pulls out a percentage (generally from 28 to 30 percent), multiplies it by your monthly income, and decrees that this is the amount you can afford to pay each month for shelter. Next he'll ask how much of a down payment you plan on shelling out, and then he'll come up with his judgment of what you can afford.

Brokers and other real estate experts will take an even easier route to determine affordability. They will ask your gross yearly income and simply multiply it by two or two and a half, then proclaim that this is the size of the mortgage you can afford. They'll add in a down payment and begin to show you homes that fit in with their analysis.

Where do these formulas come from? Banks base their rules on public records of defaults, foreclosures and the census. They take data gathered from millions of people, filter it through an incredibly strong safety net, and make a judgment that offers *them* the best chance for success, crediting you with as little as possible. Bank affordability rules are based on all the bad news and worst case scenarios they can find. A banker will sit down and compare the income and mortgage size of every defaulted home. He will then find at what income level there has rarely been a default on, let's say, a $100,000 mortgage loan, and then limit all future loans of $100,000 to borrowers who have at least that income level. Bankers will also consult data tables that estimate how much you are likely to spend on food, clothing, insurance and all the other expenses of living in order to establish a ceiling on what you can spend on shelter. Having looked at these tables, I can assure you that banks invariably overestimate your expenses. Applying formulas is obviously unfair and biased, but from their point of view it is prudent and sensible. Brokers, on the other hand, come up with the two or two and a half figure through a kind of group memory. It has no basis in the real world; it is simply a convenient old wives' tale that is easy to remember.

Banks and brokers have an inkling that their formulas are somewhat arbitrary. Most lending institutions in large urban areas are prepared to stretch the rules a bit if you make a large downpayment, if you have a good credit history or if you otherwise make a strong case for yourself. (I'll discuss with you exactly how to do that in Chapter Twelve.) But the formulas are still based on *their* evaluation of your finances, motivations and spending habits, not your own. The bank's formulas on affordability may well not prove accurate in your case. The true method of determining affordability is much more complicated, but is based on you as an individual, not you as one among the faceless millions in the most recent census. By taking stock of your financial life, and then streamlining it, you'll almost certainly be able to stretch further, and afford more than any simple bank equation might dictate.

And there is nothing that is worth the effort more than the new roof over your head. Remember: The purchase of a home is the single best financial investment you will ever make. Not only is it shelter and security, it is the first step in developing a financial net worth. And it isn't just an investment for today. It can be the key to your retirement and your financial future. The equity built up in a home, or the profit made on the sale of a home, can be the financial nest egg that insures a comfortable retirement. My mother and father thank God that they bought a home—otherwise, they could never have retired.

When they were in their fifties, I badgered them into buying a home in a suburb outside New York City. They spent $10,000. Years later, after my mother decided she couldn't take the northern winters any longer, they sold the home for $100,000. After renting for two years in a retirement community, they bought a new unit for $65,000—$15,000 in cash and the rest mortgaged. Their other funds were invested in Ginnie Maes, since investment income is now much more important to them than equity in a home. Today they enjoy a healthy income and are happy homeowners too. Their financial well-being began with the purchase of that $10,000 home.

For all these reasons, buying a home justifies a relatively high degree of sacrifice and risk. But *you* should decide how much sacrifice and risk you want to undertake—not the bank or broker.

Formulas do not work because of all the variables involved, including the most important variable of all—your personality. Affordability is to a large extent a measure of your risk aversion, and you are the only person who can calculate that factor. And believe it or not, that calculation becomes more complicated the more affluent you are. People look at affordability in terms of how things are. We'll be showing you how to look at things as they will be, which, I suggest, is a more valid measurement.

The moment when you decide to buy a home (and determine what you can afford) is the single best time in your life to undertake a thoroughgoing financial inventory. It is probably the first point in your life when you'll be acquiring a major asset, one that will radically alter your whole financial being. An entirely new set of rules, as well as a whole new set of stresses, come into play. You are going to have to analyze your finances anyway, since banks and sellers will want to check on them. Why not use this opportunity to turn over the soil of your finances, and plant the seeds of your future in fresh, fertile earth? An accurate financial inventory will not only give you a handle on how much you can actually spend on a home, it will help you reach new plateaus of affordability. At the very least, it will call your attention to some of the bad financial habits you picked up from your parents or fell into while in college.

Your affordability is the monthly amount you can pay for shelter. This figure includes principal, interest, taxes, maintenance, common charges and sometimes insurance. The number will be the product of *your* analysis. It won't be based on the preconceived notions of banks, brokers, parents, siblings or friends—it is truly a custom job. Remember, this isn't just shelter you are buying; it's also an investment, so you are going to stretch as far as you safely can.

The first thing to do is to look at every penny you spend. Most Americans can only identify where about 75 percent of their money goes. If you want to afford that home of your dreams, you'll have to get a handle on the whereabouts of that mysterious 25 percent. The first two places to look are your monthly credit card bills and those cash machine receipts stuffed into your wallet.

Credit cards are insidious. They turn purchasing into a painless pastime. Pulling a card out of your wallet and handing it to a salesperson is an abstract process. I'm convinced that credit cards actually numb the rational centers of your brain. You aren't asking yourself "Am I spending too much?" or "Do I need this now?," when you pay with plastic. Credit cards anesthetize the purchase transaction; they obliterate that reflective pause in the process which takes place when we see our dollars physically leave our wallet. In determining our home affordability, we must make every effort to be conscious of every penny we spend. Stop paying for insignificant purchases with your credit cards. Save them for big ticket items like the living room furniture, or the down payment (I'll be dealing with that a little later in this chapter).

Cash machines are another trap. They make it far too easy to get your hands on crisp $20 bills twenty-four hours a day. Start paying by check instead. Drawing a check is an analytical process. It has its share of pain, and that works as a subtle deterrent. You write down where it's going, what it's for, and then you subtract the amount from your balance. By eliminating all those expenses labelled "cash," you'll find you can cut down drastically on that unknown 25 percent of your spending.

By trimming credit card balances and cash expenses, you'll boost the amount you can spend on your shelter/investment, often by a great deal. But we're not done yet. There are still some financial skeletons in your closet that have to be exposed to the bright sunlight of financial sanity.

Take a look at your insurance. Life insurance is an obscene racket—one of the great cesspools of American finance. If you are worried about what will happen to your spouse and dependents if you die or become incapacitated, take out term (a policy that stretches over a specific period of time with an established value, payable to you, upon expiration), health or disability insurance. Calculate your life insurance needs on the basis of what it would take to keep your family on its feet for a year or two, paying all outstanding debts, and providing a college education. Insure only those members of the family who make financial contributions. Don't look at insurance as an investment—it has a disgraceful yield, nowhere near as good as that of real estate. Forget about extras like double indemnity or flight insurance, unless they are free. Take the largest deductible allowed—it's the hurricane you are worried about, not the dent in the fender. Casualty insurance should only insure you against catastrophe. I've found that you can save 20 to 30 percent by taking the highest deductible offered. If you want to provide for your heirs, do it now, when you are alive. At least you'll get some thanks and be able to see them enjoy it.

It's time to economize. Don't buy Chateau Lafite Rothschild 1961. Drink something domestic. Stop going out to dinner five nights a week. Give up smoking. Rent a videotape instead of going out to the movies. Hire an accountant to go over your tax returns with a fine-tooth comb, making sure you keep every possible penny in your own hands. Stop increasing the value of the gifts you give every year. You can blame your frugality on the house. These cutbacks should more than compensate for the increased expenses you'll have from owning a home. Eventually you'll be paid back royally. I mean this not just in monetary terms—though those aren't insubstantial—but in an improved quality of life and a renewed sense of purpose.

It can be done. I know. I've done it for myself, my children, my parents and my clients. I cut my gift expenses by 30 percent. I cut my entertainment costs by 25 percent—barbeques instead of dinner parties, movies at home instead of Broadway shows. I bought a Honda instead of a BMW. I reduced my insurance bill from $8,000 a year to $3,500, without reducing coverage. It turned out that prices had fallen since I first bought many of my policies. Insurance companies aren't going to call you up and tell you prices have dropped, and then offer you a new, cheaper policy. You have to do the investigation yourself.

Once you have taken a cold, hard look at your day-to-day spending as well as at other discretionary expenses, it's time to draw up a budget. Try to be as accurate as possible. Don't rely on your memory: Go through your check book and credit card bills. Trace where every penny is going. Your personal budget should be as exacting as that of any business. Eliminate—now—all unnecessary expenses.

How do you know if you can stick to this budget? Keep track of your performance for three months after implementing all your line item vetoes. You'll be amazed at how the simple awareness of where all your money goes will translate into substantial savings. After three months your new streamlined budget will tell you exactly how much you can afford to spend each month on "shelter," and how much you can afford to borrow.

But affordability doesn't stop there. Rent isn't tax deductible. Mortgage payments are, at least in part. As an owner, you'll receive what amounts to a subsidy from Uncle Sam, and that amount should be included in determining your affordability. Under the new tax law the interest portion of your monthly mortgage payment will be deductible at the 28 percent tax bracket. That means that if your budget says you can afford to pay $1,000 in rent, you can actually afford to pay $1,280 for a mortgage payment. That's because, in the early years of a mortgage, monthly payments consist almost entirely of interest, and thus are almost completely tax deductible. If you are patient, you can wait for your refund to make up the difference. But a better method may be to increase the number of exemptions on your W-4 tax withholding form. You'll then have more money in your paycheck to help pay that monthly mortgage bill.

In my experience, I've found that the people who stretch beyond the level of affordability dictated by the bank usually thrive. At the beginning there may be some stress and some pain. But in time everything comes together. As your priorities change, so will your spending habits. And, in all likelihood, your income will rise—while your mortgage payment stays the same. Sure there are risks, but there is no better time to take a substantial risk than now. Will you be able to convince a banker of your ability to afford more than his little equation says? Yes, because (as I'll demonstrate in Chapter Twelve) we're not simply going to fill out a mortgage application. We'll add our own supplement to show how we will be able to pay back the loan.

With that in mind, pick up a mortgage chart. Look for a reasonable interest rate—say, 10 percent. (I'll discuss the relative merits of different types of mortgages in Chapter Twelve.) Figure on a thirty-year mortgage. By working backwards with the chart, you'll find that for every $800 you can spend monthly, you can borrow $100,000. Remember that you will have to pay taxes, maintenance, common charges and insurance, as well as the interest and principal. With a mortgage total in hand, you have to move on to the next step, adding in your down payment, to determine the total price you can afford to pay for your home.

I know this sounds complicated, but it really isn't. Let's look at a hypothetical case in order to understand better the basics of affordability. Sidney Carton is paying $750 in rent each month for an apartment. Realizing that perhaps he has been living extravagantly, Sidney sits down and examines where all his money is going. After substituting subway rides for his sizable taxicab expenses, replacing breakfasts at the diner with coffee and cereal at home, and cutting out his weekly theater tickets, Sidney discovers that he can add another $250 to his shelter figure, bringing it up to $1,000.

Doing some quick calculations, Sidney sees that he falls

into the new 28 percent tax bracket. Knowing that in the first five years approximately 85 percent of his mortgage payment will be interest, he figures out that $850 of his $1,000 will be deductible. By multiplying his marginal tax bracket (28 percent) by the value of the deduction ($850), Sidney knows that he will be paying at least $238 less in taxes each month. By altering his W-4 form to allow for this new deduction, Sidney can take the money home with him right away, and add it to the amount he can afford to pay for shelter each month.

Sidney's new monthly budget for shelter is $1,238. But he knows that not all of this amount can go toward the principal and interest on his mortgage loan. From the total, he subtracts $50 for insurance, and another $100 for property taxes. Left with a monthly total of $1,088—actually $1,096.97 once he gives up his imported cigars—Sidney picks up a mortgage chart and sees that by assuming a 10 percent, thirty-year mortgage, he will be able to borrow $125,000. But Sidney doesn't stop there. To come up with the total amount he can pay for a home, he must add in his down payment—and that calls for another round of financial soul searching.

Never let the down payment be a deterrent to buying a home. The number one reason people give for not buying a house is that they can't afford a down payment. They say they are only half ready—they can handle the payments, but not the down payment. You can't be half ready to buy a house—that's like being half pregnant. You can make yourself ready. If you intuitively feel you can do it, you probably can.

Where do you get your down payment? Well, if you're lucky you have a bundle sitting in the bank. But that isn't likely in today's world. In the economy of the 1980s and 1990s you get your down payment anywhere you can. Down payments aren't looked on as the sacred things they used to be. Banks used to love to see big down payments—they viewed them as a statement of genuineness, an affirmation of your maturity, and an indication of your desire to own a home. Today, banks love to make mortgage loans. With the GI bill, which offered veterans 98 percent mortgages, the government all but admitted that down payments were overrated. They really give no true indication of your ability, or willingness, to repay a loan—and that is all the bank is really interested in.

Many people today are waiting around for their savings accounts to grow into down payments. They've got a long wait coming—quite possibly an endless one. In today's economy, with real estate prices increasing at a higher rate than salaries are, it is next to impossible to save the money for your down payment. The longer you wait, the further you will find yourself from being able to buy your home. There are other ways to get your down payment together—right now. In fact, the sources for the down payment are limited only by your imagination.

I know of someone who extended his credit cards to the limit for the 10 percent down payment the bank demanded. Conceivably, you could take out a credit card from an Arkansas bank (where interest rates are very low) and use the cash advance for your own down payment, or at least a part of it. You can go anywhere, and do anything to get the money—as long as it isn't illegal or painful. (Don't sell your blood, however. Save that for your kids' college tuition.) There is nothing un-American about borrowing for a down payment. I can help you with every other step in the process—each hurdle on the path to home ownership—but here is where you have to demonstrate your willingness to sacrifice for your future.

Don't hesitate to return to the nest for a down payment. The old notion was that once the children turned twenty-one, they were emancipated. Today's child, however, doesn't have half the financial advantages his or her parents did. Parents grew up in an inflationary economy in which values increased dramatically. The average parents are worth three times what their children will ever be worth. Don't feel any shame. There is nothing wrong with turning to your parent for help with the down payment. In America today, the family home has become the foundation of a family's wealth. Your parents' fabulous investment is your inheritance, your patrimony. Don't worry—parents are well aware of the economic situation and most are more than willing to turn over at least part of your birthright when you are buying a home, rather than when they're gone. After all, they'll be able to join in the joy of your home.

If the nest isn't still open, try prying it open. A loan from parents can be a gift, but it can also be a business transaction. Many of my clients work out investment deals with their parents, making them partners in the purchase of a home. When the home is sold the parents get a piece of the action— an "equity kicker"—just like venture capitalists do. On at least five occasions in the past year I have instructed successful, college-educated yuppies on how to approach their parents about reopening the nest for a down payment loan. Most parents are willing to help the children if you can show them how it can be done without damaging "the estate." My advice has often simply been to ask for help. Most parents delight in helping their children, especially when that help amounts to a reaffirmation of their own life-style—as home owners.

If your parents can't help out with the down payment, look for relatives and friends who would like to invest in real estate. Even your maiden aunt who is nervous about the stock market knows that a real estate investment offers unparalleled growth and security. And with you managing it, the investment is even safer. Take on a silent partner. Offer him or her 25 percent ownership of the home, while you keep the right to live in it. You'll manage the property and when it comes time to sell, your partner will receive 25 percent of the profits. Alternatively, you can form a real estate investment syndicate with five friends, each of whom kicks in capital to purchase the home. Everyone receives a share of the profit, while you retain possession. There are no hard and fast rules on how much cash you should get for giving up 25 percent. It's a judgment call best based on your relationship with the investor(s) and their financial situation.

Frame the deals according to the degree of risk appropriate to your investor's age and life-style. Obviously, your contract with your brother or sister should be different from the contract with your parents—siblings will be more likely to come in for the long haul; parents tend to prefer less equity and more interest income. Offer them a guaranteed return, perhaps 2 or 3 percent above the cost of living, and have it accrue yearly. If the agreed upon rate is 8 percent, and your parents loan you $10,000, they will make $800 in the first year. The next year, figure the 8 percent on $10,800.

Perhaps you can come up with a hybrid deal. Offer your investor a nominal rate of interest as well as a piece of the action when you sell. Spice up the deal a little by giving them an exit. Give your investors the option of pulling out after five years. At that time you can take out a second mortgage, or refinance your first mortgage, in order to pay them off.

These deals should all be made in writing, stipulating how the loan will be paid back, and what the creditor's exit is. Don't offer to pay back the principal over a period of time. Pay it back, instead, out of the proceeds from the sale. Who knows? Your parents may even forgive the debt.

Go up to the attic and look through all those possessions gathering dust. It's surprising sometimes how much your collectibles are worth. Sell the silver you got as a wedding present. Recycle the crystal into cash. Check the value of Uncle Otto's stamp collection that has sat in the drawer for forty years. Include everything. Don't worry about what your sister would say if that crystal bowl she bought you isn't sitting on the shelf anymore. Instead of a rent party or a yard sale, hold a home-buying party and sell all those items you don't need. Scour your safe deposit box for those old bonds you were given as a child. Cash them in. Forget about the annuity that you've been setting up.

Should you put all your available cash into the down payment, or save some as an emergency reserve? The answer to that question is different for everyone, depending on his or her aversion to risk. A person of seventy shouldn't assume much risk, since there is little time to recoup a loss. A forty-year-old can take a slightly greater risk. A thirty-year-old can take a great many risks, since he or she will have three or four opportunities to recoup over the course of a career. Whatever your decision, don't automatically adopt someone else's risk aversion—not your parents' and not your banker's. This is something you must figure out on your own. But keep in mind: There is no better time to take a risk than when you are buying a home.

Once you have added your down payment to the mortgage you can afford to pay back, you're left with one more calculation in order to come up with your affordability. Take your total—mortgage and down payment—and add another

20 percent to it in order to allow for the difference between asking prices and what, after negotiation, you're likely to pay. (I'll get into the fine points of negotiation in Chapter Nine, but for now, assume you'll be able to knock the asking price down 20 percent.) This is the price you'll give the broker when you start on your search for the home of your dreams.

While you should be accurate at every step in determining affordability, make sure you stretch to the limit. Remember, the worst thing that can happen is that you can't afford the home after you buy it. If that does happen, you made a mistake somewhere in your calculations, or you didn't stick to your new streamlined budget.

What to do then? Your mortgage banker is perhaps the easiest lender you'll ever bargain with. I know. I was one. The last thing he wants is your house. He'll work with you even more than that maiden aunt or that syndicate of friends will. Often the banker will work out the loan by temporarily reducing monthly payments to the interest only, or by offering a set period of payments at a reduced rate. If a banker forecloses on a home, he'll probably have to sell it at auction. You can bet he'll get a lot less for your home than you could. (The smell of a foreclosure draws the real estate vultures who are looking for a steal.) That's why bankers want the mortgage deal to work out, and will bend over backwards to help. But don't wait until you get too deep into a hole. Talk to your banker at the first sign of trouble. He'll appreciate your candor, and will probably help you work out the problem. As long as there was some communication between myself and the problem borrower, I tried my hardest to avoid any adverse actions. You need answers for your superiors as well as the bank examiners, and the best way to get both is through communication with the borrower.

There is no black-shrouded specter that will suddenly bang on your door and throw you out into the street. You'll have plenty of warning if things aren't going to work out, and there will be more than enough time to sell the home and escape. While there is often strain in meeting the monthly payments in the early years, rest assured that the pain soon eases up. Your income will more than likely increase, and you will also find that your priorities magically readjust, freeing more money for the payment. Also inflation will make your payment cheaper over a period of time. It may seem hard to believe today, but a whole variety of factors will work together to make those monthly payments more affordable as time goes on.

And even with all the stretching and reaching, we won't be foolish. We've prepared a budget, listing all our income and expenses, showing the bank how we can afford more than the standard equation dictates. Our gamble is that we can trim our expenses down to the bone, and that we can eventually add to our income. You are going to be optimistic and hopeful, not crazy. You're betting on your future. And that has to be a good wager, since the outcome depends on you, no one else. If you're afraid to bet heavily on your future, that's okay. Your lack of self-confidence—reflected in the affordability judgment you made—will merely reduce the price you can pay, not eliminate you from the market.

Regardless of the amount of risk you take on, you have to plan optimistically. You cannot live your life thinking about all the negatives that can knock on your door tomorrow. Successful generals plan to win the war, not avoid losing it. Take charge. The obstacles are inside you. Once you realize you can vault them with ease, you'll find that a wealth of opportunity awaits you.

CHAPTER SIX

LOCATION ANALYSIS

Not all that tempts your
wand'ring eyes
And heedless hearts, is lawful prize;
Nor all that glisters, gold.
THOMAS GRAY

The oldest aphorism in the real estate business holds that the three keys to any property purchase are location, location and location. Why else would two identical homes in, let's say, McKeesport, Pennsylvania, and Greenwich, Connecticut, vary by as much as fifteen times in value? While it is true that the biggest mistake you can make in purchasing a home is to buy one you cannot afford, the second biggest mistake is buying a house in the wrong location. And this mistake can't be undone simply by selling the home. By buying in a poor location you are apt to lose money when selling.

Another traditional piece of real estate advice is that "It is better to buy the worst home on a block than the best." Why? Because a mediocre house in a great location will appreciate in value faster than a dream house in a mediocre location—it has more room to rise in price since it is probably further from its ultimate price than the better home. Sometimes the best investment in a community is the cheapest. The one bedroom apartment on the twentieth floor of an apartment building will go up in price faster than the three bedroom apartment on the eighth floor. And a good investment should have the potential to increase, not just retain its value.

Let me give you a good example. I bought my current office condominium when the building was half full. The salesperson sized me up and then offered to show me the penthouse apartment. I told him that instead, I wanted something dark on the lowest floor available. Not only did I get the condo at my price, but it is inching up in value much more rapidly than the penthouse they originally wanted to show me.

Even though our primary motivation in buying a home is to find wonderful space to live in, our secondary—yet still essential—consideration should be to make an intelligent, profitable investment. A good job of location analysis helps you predict the future better than any crystal ball. The purchase of a home is probably the single largest investment you will ever make. Doing the best scouting job possible will help insure that you invest wisely. In fact, a sound location analysis will turn every dollar you invest today into $10 when you sell.

But it won't be easy to analyze location. No broker or seller is going to volunteer the information that the empty lot next door is slated to become a toxic waste dump. Brokers are notorious for taking you on the scenic route to see a property. They'll drive past the park, the restaurants, the schools and the library, pointing each out to you, and then pull up to the home. All those lovely sights and amenities make their positive impressions and become associated with the house. If you had taken the most direct route you might have driven past the paint factory and the halfway house—not the idyllic scenes the broker or seller wants to plant in your mind.

This past year I was hired by the vice president of finance for a major international conglomerate to look at a condo apartment for him and his wife. In the past, this man had exhibited remarkable financial shrewdness, but lousy real estate acumen. He had bought and sold homes four times in four different states in the past thirty years, and each time took a loss. He was determined to see that this wouldn't happen to him in New York City and therefore sought me out. The apartment of his dreams was a model apartment. Its true dimensions were obscured by mirrors and artistic lighting. Still, it was a wonderful apartment. Then I stepped out on the balcony. I saw a wonderful, unobstructed view of downtown Manhattan. Unfortunately, the model was on the twenty-fourth floor and when I looked down to the ground I saw that next door was a vacant lot. I knew that vacant lots in that part of Manhattan are only temporarily vacant. And once they are built on will stretch as high as the law allows, thus obstructing that magnificent view.

I have been in the car with brokers who keep up a charming patter as they drive me along a beautiful route to a property for sale. Once I express lack of interest in the property I'm driven back in half the time along a singularly unscenic route. I was guilty of a similar practice myself back when I sold commercial properties on New York's Long Island. Buyers were invariably concerned about travel time to the site, so I would make sure to show the properties only at times when traffic would be sparse.

Location is so vital that I advise my clients to scout locations first, before looking at specific homes. By doing a little preliminary research, you can test the integrity of brokers and builders. You'll also avoid the trap of falling in love with a dream house in a dump location. Brokers and sellers know that the first impression you have is the most lasting, and they'll do their utmost to manipulate it. Remember: You are going to stop yourself from falling in love with the home, at least until you move in. Location analysis must be a deliberate, coldly objective act on the buyer's part. Don't rely on any outside parties for an accurate judgment on the quality of a location.

Builders and, surprisingly, even bankers, are unreliable sources of information about location. Experienced builders buy land for the future and stockpile it. They may have started building a development just because the land mortgage came due. Builders are expert at marketing and will do everything possible to obscure an area's problems. And don't assume that, just because a bank is willing to write an attractive mortgage on a property, the financial institution has deemed the home a great investment. The developer may have enticed the bank by *buying down* mortgages—paying a sizable fee to the bank so that the mortgage has an artificially attractive interest rate. Bankers can become as overzealous as home buyers when a good-looking deal is waved in front of their eyes. And the banker, builder and broker don't have to live there. They'll go home to their upscale neighborhoods, leaving you next to the community dump.

The area's chamber of commerce spends most of its time and money trying to obscure any problems with the community, so it isn't going to be a source of unbiased information. Even your potential next-door neighbors won't have a bad word to say about their town, block or building. After all, they live there. They have an interest in keeping real estate values as high as possible. And who knows? They may be very anxious to get rid of the current neighbor and his pet pit bull.

No, location analysis is something you'll have to do on your own. Some of the information can be bought. But you are the person who is investing in the home. It's your money and your life that will be tied up in this purchase. No one else has the expertise and motivation to do the job right.

A good rule of thumb is that if values in a community are rising, they will in all likelihood continue to do so. If they are flat, or falling, they will also continue to do so. But beyond this general examination, there are a whole series of investigations you will have to perform to get a true reading on a location.

The first step is the simplest. If you are looking at an urban neighborhood, lace up your sneakers. Is your home of the future in the suburbs? Then fill up the gas tank of your car. You're about to go on your first reconnaissance mission.

Real estate speaks to you; it tells you of its health. All you have to do is listen. Most of us walk or drive through neighborhoods and towns all the time, and never really see what is going on. A couple of years ago a client asked me to look into a PUD (planned unit development) in Puerto Rico. There I was, unable to speak the language, scouting in an area where I couldn't communicate with anyone. Still, I could tell what was happening. I could see how well property was being cared for. I saw that every businessman and merchant were dressed in shirt and tie. Homeowners were literally scrubbing their sidewalks and front steps. The area shouted its vitality. I could see it in the attitude of the waiters at the country club my host had taken me to, in the manners of the desk clerk at the hotel I was staying in, and in the smile of the cab driver who drove me around. You can sense success as long as you don't cloud your eyes and ears with urgency or wish fulfillment.

On your trip through a location, you'll have to keep all five senses as alert as possible in order to experience and absorb all there is to learn. To sharpen your senses, ask yourself questions:

What do the buildings or houses look like? Are they well taken care of—are the lawns manicured, walls clean of dirt and grime? What makes and years of cars are parked in front of the homes? Are they new, or at least in good shape? Is there garbage on the street or sidewalk? Are there sidewalks at all? Are the streetlights working? Is the area predominantly residential or are there offices, warehouses and factories as well? Are there doormen polishing brass rails or supers guzzling beer by the front door? A manicured, well cared for town is indicative of a healthy, vibrant community.

A town should have a healthy heart. Look for an active

prosperous main street. If there's no main street, there's something missing from the town or neighborhood. Check for statues and monuments. You can tell a lot about a community by whom and what it chooses to honor.

The business district of a community speaks volumes to the acute observer. Look for a store that is just opening. What type of store is it, and what preceded it? If it's a gourmet food shop replacing a luncheonette, the town or neighborhood is probably on the way up. If the reverse is true, start worrying.

Think about your daily shopping needs, and look for grocery stores, pharmacies and dry cleaners. Go into a few stores. Are they busy? What are the prices like? Look at the inventory in the stores. Is it fresh and clean? If a layer of dust coats the wares, then it's safe to assume that the store, and possibly also the town, are on the down side of the slope. Are the window displays yellowed? No store that has an active business is going to have its Christmas decorations up in February. If the owner is sitting down, reading a newspaper, you can bet you aren't on Little Fifth Avenue.

Check out the stores' hours. A healthy town or neighborhood will have long business hours. Stores that are doing well won't close for lunch—they'll be able to afford as many employees as are necessary to stay open straight through the day, and part of the evening too. If you see a florist shop closed on Sunday, the community probably isn't thriving. Shopping centers that are deserted on a Thursday after five are never going to be crowded. Go to the local supermarket. Read the notices on the bulletin board. Talk to the manager. I've found that supermarket chains tend to put their worst managers in the worst towns, making sure they won't screw up good stores. Look for a local Kiwanis or Lions club. Any town that has an active, cooperative business community is healthy.

Besides having an active business community, a vibrant town or neighborhood will also have a certain level of cultural awareness. Is there a museum or movie house nearby? How about a video rental store? Are there people out and about at night? What are they doing with their leisure time?

In the residential areas, is there clothing hanging out on lines? Do you see bicycles and toys lying around, or does it seem like there isn't a child within ten miles? How far is it to the primary and secondary school, and what will the walk be like for your kids? How many vacant lots are there in the immediate area? Do you see signs of future building projects, or are the lots simply abandoned? Are there "for sale" signs on homes?

Although a community—whether a suburban town or urban block—is a complicated organism, many judgments can be made simply by examining its surface carefully and the walking or driving tour should provide a wealth of valuable insight. But to get the full picture of a community you'll have to dig a bit deeper.

I'm often asked to check into locations for clients. What I do is call the local utilities, the chamber of commerce and the regional tourist bureau, and ask for all the information they have on the area. While the information is often biased, outright lies are rare and it's usually easy to extract the facts from the hype.

If I'm scouting for real estate in a small town, I next call a local banker and make an appointment to meet with him. I say that I am interested in creating a relationship with the town and his bank. I ask him for information on the town's government and its plans. The banker, anxious to get my business, invariably goes out of his way to be helpful. I ask how long the current administration has been in office, and whether they are full- or part-time politicians. I try to ask factual questions, rather than ones that call for his opinions. In that way, I can make my own judgments, rather than rely on the banker's analysis. I ask for the name of the best broker in town. I discuss with the banker how long it is taking for homes to turn over, how many new businesses have started, how many have closed, and what the vacancy rate is for commercial property. I'll check into what he feels are the best, and worst areas of town. I ask him whether taxes are on the way up, moving down or stable.

More than likely, the banker will arrange introductions to a handful of important figures in the community—local lawyers, the school superintendent, a utility company's representative and, of course, a a real estate broker. The broker then rolls out the red carpet for me, driving me around town, buying me coffee, offering his insights into the town. While this information is often tainted by salesmanship, important information can nonetheless be gleaned by again asking factual questions. I ask the broker what the most expensive part of town is, how long it is taking for homes to sell and how far apart the asking and selling prices are as a rule.

I pick up copies of the local newspapers. Skipping the news pages, I turn to the classified ads—they often tell you more about what is going on in town. I look at the help-wanted ads and, of course, the real estate ads. Locations with more than one local newspaper are either unusually healthy, or unusually political. Since many local tabloids are boosters for the town, you want to find a paper that is objective. There is one trick to determining if the paper is objective: if it publishes the police blotter you can bet it's more than just a mouthpiece for the town government and chamber of commerce.

The investment that is closest to my heart is my summer home on Martha's Vineyard in Massachusetts. Unfortunately, I can't spend all my time there. How do I keep track of my cherished investment? I subscribe to the *Vineyard Gazette*. By reading the paper I can keep my finger on the pulse of the community. New stores advertise grand opening specials, and dying stores publicize going out of business sales. Proposed zoning variances are reported—and by taking note of which ones pass and which ones are defeated, I can keep track of the local government's policies. Crimes, from break-ins and drunk driving to drug busts and homicides, are reported in the weekly police blotter. I can deduce trends in property values from the real estate ads. Through the local newspaper I can keep an eye on my investment from 250 miles away.

Pay particularly close attention to the zoning and land use plans of the community. In an urban area, that means the block and the surrounding two or three blocks on all sides. In suburbia it means the entire town or village. Check for vacant lots or buildings about to be demolished. You can assume that any empty lot will be put to the highest and most profitable use by a developer. That means whatever is built there will be as high and wide as the law allows—and sometimes it will be even higher and wider. If a home you are interested in has windows overlooking an empty lot, you can assume there will be a brick wall there in the near future.

My Uncle Jack used to be considered the real estate expert in the family. He and his wife worked hard all their lives and finally bought a beautiful retirement home—a picturesque cottage on a little peninsula jutting out into the Hudson River. Surrounded on three sides by water, Uncle Jack planned on spending his golden years in glorious contemplation of nature. Unfortunately, he woke up one morning and found that they had started to build the Tappan Zee Bridge almost directly over his picture post card cottage. Of course the seller and the broker didn't warn him. Even the people in town didn't talk about it—maybe they thought that by not discussing it, it wouldn't happen. But there had been a way for Uncle Jack to find out about the town's future plans for his retirement paradise.

The attitude of the local government toward development can play a large role in the values of homes. Some municipalities look to grow. They encourage developers and are apt to issue a great many variances and tax breaks. If you are going to be starting a business in town, that can be a marvelous advantage. But if you are looking for a refuge from the city's chaos, it can be dangerous.

A quick trip to the local planning or building department will reveal all the plans a town or city has for the future. The future is of vital concern to every community, whether they are looking to grow, or to avoid growth. You'll find maps of proposed roads, power lines, housing developments and industrial parks. Commercial and industrial developments are beneficial for home owners, since they help absorb the cost of community services without drawing their share of the school or park advantages. Still, you don't want them going up next door. See if the city or town has a master plan. If they don't, that could mean that developers have a free hand to do whatever they will. On the other hand, it could mean that the town is as developed as it ever will be, and no further growth or building is being planned. Visit the local utilities, the power and telephone companies. Tell them you are interested in relocating to the area. They'll have reams of data on future energy users—new factories, shopping centers, industrial parks, large residential developments—as well as projections on long-term energy demands owing to growth or shrinkage in the town or neighborhood.

What is the weather and climate like in the area? Local newspapers usually keep records of the highs and lows in temperature, snow fall and rain. Check with insurance agents and see if the area is a flood risk. Never ask the chamber of commerce for information on climate. They'll tell you about the ninety-nine straight days of sun, and fail to tell you that there were also ninety-nine straight days of 100-degree temperature. Climate can strongly effect the property values in a community. In certain areas of the country, cities and towns become desolate in the summer or the winter, as residents flee extreme temperatures for the moderate climates. Some places suffer from annual invasions of insects. At the same time, take a look for any specific environment problems that a particular area might have. Call the local department of health and ask about water quality and availability. Local environmental groups can alert you to potential environmental problems. Different regions have their own hidden time bombs (in the Colorado River area it might be lack of water; in New Jersey it might be radon contamination).

What is the economic base of the community? It's important that the area have a healthy industrial or commercial foundation. Otherwise homeowners will be alone in footing the tax bill for services. But make sure that the economic base is comprised of a variety of industries, and that they are stable. Those parts of the country that were dependent on single industries—automaking, steel, oil—have become ghost towns when their principal business fell on hard times. Look at Detroit, or the Monongahela Valley in Western Pennsylvania. While there may be pockets of good and bad areas in any town, its overall health depends on a stable economic base. One of the reasons the Northeast has continued to prosper is that it is home to a service economy today—finance, media and high technology—that is more diversified and therefore not as volatile as the industrial economies of the Rust Belt.

Call your stock broker and find out what the Moody's

investment rating is for the municipality. Think twice if the community's bonds aren't A-rated. Get the full report from the broker and read it carefully. It will contain both a history of the municipality's past finances, and projections on the future.

Check out the attitude of the local government toward services. Is there a full-time professional police department, or are there two semi-retired cops? Check into the fire department. Is it professional or volunteer? Are the police cars, fire trucks, official buildings and other municipal properties in good shape? If not, taxes will be on the way up. Does the community provide garbage collection, or will you have to pay for your own? Is there a town dump which you will have access to if you have to take care of your own disposal, or will you have to pay for a carting service? Is there a sewer system, private septic or a combination of both? Many towns charge a sewer tax, or a fee for connecting your home to new sewers. If the town is in the process of adding a sewer system, you can count on broken-up, muddy streets for at least a year. Is water included in your property tax bill, or is there a separate charge depending on your level of usage? What is the water quality? Taste it. If your water is free but undrinkable, you'll have to pay for a private water service.

An enlightened, professional local government can do a great deal to enhance property values. Some governments work at making their town a better place to live. For example, does the government sponsor senior citizen programs and activities for teens and children?

Look for a full-time professional government. The trend today is toward city managers (trained professionals), as opposed to elected officials, who are often little more than the winners of local popularity contests. Read the newspapers for hints about the competence of the government, and stay away from any place that doesn't smell quite right. A good way to check up on local government is by calling the state legislature for the area. States rate their municipalities in hundreds of ways—by money spent per pupil, by taxes generated, by expenditures for roads and libraries. Every time state government invests money in an area, it keeps track of it, safeguarding residents from the potential abuses of the local officials. Ask the legislator, or his staff, to send you this sort of information.

Find out from the tax assessor's office what the assessment rate is in the community, and where it is headed. There is a trend in the U.S. toward 100 percent assessment—states are mandating that local municipalities bring their property taxes up to date, rather than apply for more state aid. Any community that is on the road to reassessment (or 100 percent equalization) could see its taxes double.

Is education of vital importance to you? Even if not, the schools can tell you a lot. Remember, the best towns tend to attract the best teachers, and therefore, have the best school systems. Besides checking out the proximity of schools in your first tour of the area, take a look at the educational values of the community.

The state department of education can provide you with the student/teacher ratio for every community, as well as tell you how much financial aid has been given to the school district on a per pupil basis.

Talk to a member of the school board—anyone on the board is bound to be zealous about the schools, and more than willing to discuss them. Ask whether the school population is growing or shrinking, and how that fits in with the number of schools already in existence. A community with few schools, but with a growing student population, will have to raise taxes in the near future. A shrinking student population means that fewer teachers will have to be hired, and that school buildings might be rented out, lessening the tax bite on residents. Find out if children are bused, and if so, whether this is done to balance area or racial biases. How are the school children grouped together? Schools that contain a wide range of ages may spell trouble. Look at the area's students' ratings on standardized tests, such as the SAT exam. While these tests aren't an infallible indicator, they can give some idea of the level of instruction. Ask what percentage of high school students graduate, and what percentage go on to college.

Check to see where school districts spend their money. Does the budget stress computers for elementary school students, or new uniforms for the cheerleading squad? Ask for a tour of the educational facilities and see where the community's priorities lie. Make an appointment to meet the school's principal. Your judgment of him can go a long way in telling you about the school over which he presides.

Sit in on a class for a firsthand look at the quality of education. I never realized how valuable that could be until, as I mentioned earlier, my wife sat in on second and third grade classes at a renowned public school in a Manhattan neighborhood we had moved into. She came away disappointed and unhappy. The classes were no better than the schools on Long Island, whose main claim to fame was turning out dental technicians and sending students to schools of hotel and restaurant management so they could help with daddy's business.

Find out what special programs and courses are offered. Look for a school that stresses reading and writing. Computers are nice, but books are better. Go to a PTA meeting. Listen to the topics discussed. See how many parents show up. A low turnout means an uninterested community.

See if there is a library in the area. Towns that choose not to fund a library can't be too serious about the education of their children. Is there a college or university nearby? Besides offering advantages for your offspring, a nearby institution of higher learning can add a great deal to the quality of your own life. A local college or university means theatrical performances. They also offer continuing education classes, which often can provide a boost to your career, or help you pursue your hobbies.

Consider the cultural outlets in the area. Is there a theater group, or a historical society? Are there concerts? Does the city have a symphony orchestra? Communities with traditions of cultural support are well established and have a proven identity. Culture tends to be the whipped cream of a community—it is the topping that is added after all the other needs have been met.

What are the recreation facilities of the community like? Are there public golf courses, tennis courts and parks? How has the community treated its recreation areas? Are they well cared for and clean, or are they littered with beer cans and overgrown weeds? Recreation budgets are often the first to be cut when times get tough, and can therefore be an indicator of the community's overall health.

Every time an appraiser does a "writing" on a property, he begins his analysis with four or five pages of demographic and psychographic analysis of the community. By consulting with an appraiser—perhaps paying him or her for an hour's time or for the introduction to a recent appraisal in the area—you can obtain a wealth of information on what your potential neighbors are like.

Demographics are the hard data about the area's residents: age, family size, average income, socioeconomic status and so on. The appraiser's report will compare the residents of the area with national averages drawn from the most recent U.S. census. It will also point out trends on the "graying," or aging of the community. Are younger people moving in? What are the most desired types of new and old homes for the area's residents? The appraiser's report will tell you. Psychographics consist of more sociological data: What newspapers do residents read? What movies do they go to? What books do they read? What is their level of education? The appraisal will also discuss the climate, economic base, topography (elevation), transportation systems, utilities, population trends, educational institutions, tax situation and even the soil quality of the community.

Don't overlook or underestimate any potential sources for information. I've found cab drivers to be a great resource in my investigative tours. Even the airport can tell you something about the town or city. Is it crowded and undergoing expansion? Or is it empty and underused? A wonderful airport was built in Monticello, New York, to bring life to a dying community. It became a model failure—a beautiful facility with no traffic. Airport traffic is a good indicator of the health of the regional economy.

Stewardesses often know more about the housing situation in a town than the real estate brokers. A few years ago I was advising some clients on residential property in a Texas city. On one trip down there I struck up a conversation with a couple of stewardesses who lived in the city. They told me that landlords were so desperate that they were offering two months rent free to new tenants. The stewardesses were moving every six months to take advantage of the landlords' desperation—getting six months' housing for four months' rent. What's the moral of this story? Simply that every thing you see, every person you talk to, every conversation you overhear, can help you analyze a location.

In all your discussions with bankers, brokers, school officials and even neighbors, try to ask questions that lead to discussion, not defensiveness. For example, it's better to ask a specific question about the school curriculum, than to ask if the schools are any good. The first question elicits a response and then leads to conversation. The second question will almost always be answered positively. Ask about a particular club or social organization in town, rather than what the neighbors are like. Ask about the quality of a specific restaurant, not simply if there are any good restaurants in town. You'll get the specific information you're looking for a lot quicker if you ask specific questions.

Location analysis is an art more than a science. It requires you to open your eyes, ears and even nostrils wider than ever before. Look at everything in terms of how it affects property values. Remember, no one else is concerned about your investment. You are alone out there. Take control. It's your responsibility to investigate the soundness of your investment in a home. And do it *before* you start looking at houses. The Taj Mahal wouldn't be worth a plug nickel if it were located in a slum. A dilapidated shack in Beverly Hills would be a much wiser investment.

CHAPTER SEVEN

ASSEMBLING THE TEAM

In for a penny, in for a pound.
W. S. GILBERT

Quite often, I run into people whose heads are full of information acquired by reading books, magazines and newspaper articles about real estate.

They recount how, on the advice of an "expert" author or a "friendly" broker, they went into the real estate war without a team of professionals on their side. Most often, real estate how-to books are written not by real estate experts, but by how-to book experts. These how-to experts often encourage the reader to become a do-it-yourselfer, in order to save professional fees. And real estate brokers, no matter how friendly, represent the seller. Invariably, these home hunters proceed to tell me horror stories about how their deals were screwed up—for want of professional advice.

By reading the chapters in this book that follow you'll acquire some expertise on each professional's area. While this won't make you an expert real estate attorney, a seasoned accountant or a veteran house inspector, it will nevertheless teach you what questions to ask. I can't make you an expert foot soldier in the battle for your home, but I can teach you to be a knowledgeable general, leading loyal and eager troops.

I've specialized in real estate law and financial advising for over thirty-five years, but I became a true expert only when I developed a reverence and respect for the expertise of others. I advise my clients to hire other professionals, and I myself hire professionals for my own real estate transactions.

Anyone who is in the market to buy a home—which may cost from $100,000 to $1 million—and who is apt to spend another $10,000 or more redecorating, and $4,000 in title insurance and points to the bank—would be foolish to cut corners when the time comes to hire the professionals. Yet almost invariably, professional fees are overlooked in tabulating the costs of buying a home. Sometimes I am amazed at how sophisticated people will quibble about professional fees. The vice president of a brokerage house will spend more time analyzing my bill than the terms of the contract for his million dollar apartment. The services rendered by a professional are often psychic in nature and for that reason their value is harder to calculate. But when you are acquiring the largest asset of your life, it is important to realize your own limitations and the value of professional assistance.

Consumers forget that the purchase of a home is not a docile transaction. Capitalism—and particularly the sale of real estate for a profit—is complicated and contentious. The real estate transaction is never simply an exchange of cash for goods. The buyer is subject to constant buffeting from outside forces. The seller, the banker and the broker are pushing, prodding and cajoling you to take an action, to do something that benefits them, not you. The decisions you will be making demand all the intelligence you possess, and quite a few areas of expertise that are beyond your reach. Even though there is a preponderance of forms available for real estate transactions, the successful purchase requires professionals to do more than fill in a couple of lines, despite the claims of brokers to the contrary. Real estate brokers are trying to create a supermarket mentality in the mind of the purchaser and seller. Don't let them get away with it. Real estate transactions should always be custom deals.

There are simply too many details in a real estate transaction for one person, or even two, to handle effectively. No general enters battle alone. Neither should you.

Nor does a general go into battle with troops hand-picked by the enemy. Yet a majority of the professionals used by home buyers today have been suggested by the real estate broker. The broker, at best, represents the deal itself. He or she receives a fee only if the home is sold. At worst, the broker represents only the interests of the seller. He or she may spend ten hours a day driving you around, showing you homes and buying you coffee. But don't fall victim to their advances. They are spies from the enemy camp—the double agents of the real estate transaction—seducing you at the same time as they serve the interests of the seller.

Brokers routinely encourage buyers either to bypass professionals—arguing that the deal is so simple it needs no professional involvement—or to select only those professionals who "won't screw up the deal." A glance at the massive Rolodex sitting on the broker's desk will reveal phone numbers of hundreds of attorneys who give only rudimentary attention to contracts, hack accountants who spend their days in store fronts filling out tax forms, inspectors who aren't looking to make waves and engineers whose eyesight is less than 20/20.

Since your Rolodex probably isn't brimming with names of first-rate lawyers, accountants, appraisers, insurance brokers, inspectors and engineers, a little scouting and research is necessary.

The professionals you want on your side should have no financial stake in the consummation of the deal. They should charge on an hourly basis or a single flat fee for services rendered. They should not have their fees tied to whether or not you ultimately buy the home. Your team of professionals must be free to discourage you from purchasing the home in question. Their advice should be based on what is in your best interest—after all, they are working for you.

The single best way to find a professional is through personal recommendation from someone in a financial bracket similar to your own who has just gone through the same process. Ask your friends and coworkers which lawyers they used for the purchase of their homes. Call your cousin who just bought an inner-city condo and ask for the name of his accountant. Call the local professional associations and ask for recommendations, stressing that you are looking for someone with expertise in real estate in general, or in the particular region in which you are buying. Compile a list of at least three potential lawyers, accountants, appraisers and so on. Avoid professionals who advertise. Lawyers and accountants who take out ads in the yellow pages do it because they need to.

The next step in hiring of professionals may initially seem presumptuous, but in fact is essential: you should interview each potential member of your team. You are ultimately responsible for the competence of your team members. While you will be in command during the purchase process, your pros will have to be there when you need them, fully prepared. The best troops will need only a nudge from you to charge into action. A whip won't be enough to prod incompetent, uncaring professionals forward. You can't afford to wait until the heat of battle before finding out which kind you've retained.

Call up each professional on your list and make an appointment to interview him or her. Many professionals are reluctant to undergo an interview with a potential client. If that's the case, ask for a free initial consultation. The pro still objects? Scratch him or her off your list. The members of your team should possess special traits that can be exhibited only in person. Don't settle for a brief telephone conversation— you wouldn't interview a babysitter over the phone, and the choice of a professional is nearly as important. It's impossible to tell if someone is understanding and concerned over the telephone. In addition, by interviewing your prospective troops at their own offices, you can see how organized their operation is and how seriously each professional takes himself and his practice. If the pro objects, citing his busy schedule, don't bother trying to squeeze fifteen minutes out of him. Anyone too busy to set time aside to talk to a prospective client isn't going to jump at your command when the game is afoot. Your professionals must be ready to do their part within twenty-four or thirty-six hours of your orders.

Any traits that the pro exhibits during the interview that turn you off will more than likely turn off everyone else who comes in contact with that pro—and that means the seller, the seller's attorney, the broker and your banker. Any negative traits evident in your pro will effect your deal negatively.

Your professionals should be full-timers, not moonlighting employees looking to pick up a few extra dollars. A full-time professional will have an office and an appearance that inspire confidence. They are the product, and the packaging—a professional manner and a well-groomed appearance—indicates a great deal about his or her self-image and seriousness.

If professionals take phone calls while you are sitting in their office, you can rest assured that they'll be doing the same when you're on pins and needles waiting for a response to your urgent inquiry.

Diplomas may be a dime a dozen, but certificates from established professional associations, and commendations from peer groups indicate a member of the profession who is respected and admired. Ask about the professional's commitment to ongoing education. No one, no matter how experienced, can keep up with the constant stream of technological and legal developments without constant refresher courses and updates.

Look for someone who expresses and demonstrates interest in your situation. Even a busy pro shows interest in his clients—indeed, that's why he's busy in the first place. No one who is good at his profession is in it solely for the money. Your professionals should, and must, inspire trust.

Tell the professionals what you'll expect from them. Tell the attorney that you will be looking for an adviser, not just a contract scribe. Inform the accountant that you will want advice in determining affordability and—if you are buying a co-op or condo—an analysis of the corporation's financial statements. Brokers must be made aware that you will expect them to represent the deal, not just the seller. Appraisers, inspectors, and engineers must be willing to jump into action within twenty-four hours of your signal. If the professional balks, find someone else. Don't hire anyone who won't accept your conditions. If they say they'll try to squeeze you into their busy schedule, find someone else—your interests are too important to be squeezed.

The secret question in any conversation with a professional is "why?" Professionals are used to answering "how?," and not getting into discussions about the reasons behind a course of action. Any pro who isn't willing to tell you why he or she does something, isn't going to work wholeheartedly for you. He or she will be looking to go his or her own way with little input and prodding from the client. Ask why a process takes the specified amount of time. Find out why the professional's fee is the stated amount. Any time a professional says that the standard procedure is so and so, ask why. Don't shy away from the pro who says he doesn't know the answer to a question but will find out. That's a plus. It shows honesty and a willingness to serve you.

Listen carefully to the professional's answers to your questions. Are they well thought out, or pat, clichéd responses? Does the professional present options, or simply state that this is the way he or she does things? Do you get the feeling that the pro will be able to put your point across effectively in a negotiation?

If at any point in the interview you discover that the professional has lied to or deceived you, leave.

Make sure that your professionals are experienced. When I was thirty-five I wouldn't have said experience is essential.

But I now realize how much I didn't know when I was thirty-five. Only years later, after going through almost every possible joy and calamity that real estate transactions can hold, can I truly call myself experienced. True expertise only comes from experiencing a variety of deals firsthand. And firsthand experience only comes with time. I've seen veteran inspectors stand outside a home, close their eyes and reflect back on their thirty-year catalog of home inspections. They'll take a deep breath and regale you with tales of similar homes' problems and blessings. None of the important elements of the home-buying transaction are learned in law school or accounting school. They can only be learned by doing. While it may sound old-fashioned, age and experience are important, even essential, in a professional.

Ask how long they have been in their field. Find out what percentage of their business involves residential real estate. Query them on how many transactions they have been involved with in the particular area you've settled on. In all this questioning, try to elicit specific answers. Any evasiveness or indecision on the part of the professional may indicate that his estimation of his own experience and expertise is on shaky ground.

The last topic you'll tackle in your interview is the professional's fee. It's okay to negotiate price with a professional. Don't accept claims of industry-wide fees and minimum standards. Your purchase of a home is a custom job—and so are the professional fees that go along with it.

Professionals are sometimes embarrassed to discuss their fees. They don't want to lose a potential client, but they also don't want to lower their rates. Try to keep from characterizing the fee as too high, or saying that the services "aren't worth it." By criticizing the price you are attacking the person. You don't want to make them feel that by reducing the price they are reducing themselves. Address price questions as if they were your problem, not the professionals'. Ask them how you can afford their fees. In fact, you are asking for professional advice. Depersonalize the issue of price. Remember, professionals tend to have rather large egos. Don't chisel. Treat the pro with respect. Let him stay in his ivory tower, just as long as you get your terms. Often he will offer to reduce the fee by eliminating some services. Usually these are unessential, and the trade-off is merely a way for the professional to rationalize the lowering of his fee. Try to get a ceiling on hours and a commitment from the pro to keep the hours "lean."

Before you leave the professionals' office, ask for the names and telephone numbers of their last three home-buying clients. By arbitrarily picking the last three transactions the pro has handled, you can avoid references who are simply shills.

Make it your business to call all three contacts. During your telephone conversation with each, assume the role of a journalist. Ask for factual responses, rather than opinions. When checking up on an attorney, ask how long it took for calls to be returned. Ask how long the contract negotiation took. Find out if the attorney was present at the closing. Or did he send an associate? If you are investigating an accountant's performance, find out how thoroughly he looked into the prospectus of co-ops or condos. Always try to phrase your questions to elicit hard information, not judgments. Most people will offer positive opinions when asked for a reference—it's the easiest course to follow. You are looking for an accurate reading on the pro's abilities and level of caring. Caring doesn't mean that the pro has to love you. Rather he should be concerned with your well-being and success as a matter of professional ethics. The pro who would make a good friend doesn't necessarily make a good team member. In fact, I prefer professionals who don't act like your friend, but are instead businesslike.

There are specific techniques for finding each type of professional you'll need, as well as certain things to look for in each potential team member:

THE ATTORNEY

A good attorney can be your second-in-command in the battle for the home. A poor one can spell disaster.

Hire an attorney as soon as you decide to begin the home-buying process. Far too many people wait until contract time to hire an attorney. At that point, many of the most crucial decisions—decisions in which the attorney can be an invaluable aid—have already been made. Your real estate lawyer should be there from day one, when you are deciding how much you can afford to spend, and where you will be looking for a home. The attorney can be a valued adviser at every step in the process.

You want a personal relationship with your lawyer. For that reason, I advise that you stay away from a large law firm. The large firms departmentalize every aspect of a transaction, dividing the work among several associates and paralegals. Firms prefer that your relationship is with the firm itself, not a particular attorney. You want someone who will see the deal through and then show up at the closing and contract signing. Attorneys from large firms may send an associate or, worse yet, a paralegal to the closing. If any associates are going to be involved in your home purchase, make sure that you check into their credentials and expertise as well. You can be frank and ask whether the attorney really has the time to handle your "customized" transaction personally.

Your attorney should be a real estate specialist. Every lawyer who owns his own home considers himself a real estate expert—erroneously. You must make sure your second-in-command is a true specialist. Check with local bar associations and ask who serves on the real estate committee. These attorneys will be prime candidates for your team, or at least good sources of referrals for real estate attorneys. A real estate specialist will be more than just a scrivener filling out forms. He or she will be a good businessman as well as an astute attorney. The lawyer must have good interpersonal skills and be a supreme negotiator. Ask how long the attorney has been specializing in real estate and how many transactions similar to yours he or she has handled.

Despite what brokers may tell you, every real estate transaction should involve an attorney. Even though many states employ forms that allow the broker to handle the funds and negotiations it is essential that the buyer have a legal adviser looking on. Never sign anything without speaking to your lawyer, regardless of what the broker says. If the forms are standard, that's fine. But form companies write forms, not lawyers. You are not buying off the rack.

As I will point out in later chapters on negotiation and contracts, real estate deals are often an elaborate mosaic. These deals combine creative financing, an exchange of goods in addition to cash, an elaborate set of mutual obligations as well as issues of timing and so on. Your purchase is going to be a custom job—one that requires a lawyer's skills and creativity.

Your lawyer must possess a wide range of skills: he needs to be an accomplished negotiator, a source of other experts and professionals, a financial adviser on mortgages and co-op and condo information, contract representative and closing supervisor. In addition, your attorney should be organized and appear so. He should talk practically, present a good appearance, act maturely, and be caring. If you are contemplating the purchase of a co-op or condo, your attorney should in addition have the specialized skills required to analyze the financial status of the building corporation and to make an evaluation of maintenance and common area charges.

Other pros often consider the attorney an obstacle to the deal. All the better. A competent attorney will advise you to walk out on a deal if that is in your best interest. I've found that in most cases, if a deal falls apart, it's because there was something fundamentally wrong with it, not because the attorney was obstructionist.

Real estate attorneys generally charge on an hourly basis—from $100 to $250 an hour. Arrange to have your attorney bill you on a regular basis (weekly or monthly) so that you can keep track of the fees, rather than be surprised by one tremendous bill at the end of the transaction. Ask whether you will be billed for phone calls and paralegals' time. Find out if the associates' time will be billed at a lower rate than the attorney's. You can figure your attorney will bill you for between four and six hours.

THE ACCOUNTANT

Too many people see the accountant once a year only. The purchase of a home is an excellent time to begin an ongoing relationship with an accountant. You are hiring someone who will be part of your financial life all year long, not just at tax time, when it is usually too late for him to do you much good anyway. Hire an accountant as soon as you've made the decision to buy your own home. An astute accountant can open up a world of options to you when discussing affordability. The tax ramifications of any sizable purchase must be examined prior to the purchase, especially if the house is both a shelter and an investment.

An accountant may be essential in the purchase of cooperative or condominium homes. A good one will be able to predict future maintenance costs and examine the financial structure of the corporation in under two hours. In every home purchase, an astute accountant will be able to predict and prepare for all the tax implications of a real estate purchase.

Make sure your accountant is a certified public accountant (CPA). There is no law that says a tax preparer or auditor has to be a CPA, but you want a professional who has some accountability, who has something to fear if he is negligent or unethical. In the case of a CPA, that fear is the loss of his license. This fiduciary responsible is what separates the professionals from the part-timers. Again, make sure that the accountant will be handling your principle business personally. If any work will be delegated to staff members, ask about their fees and qualifications.

Also, any accountant used in the home-buying transaction should be experienced in real estate. Accountants learn little about taxes, co-ops, condos or home affordability in professional school. Accounting schools teach debits and credits, nothing else.

Your accountant should charge on an hourly basis—between $75 and $150 per hour. As with the attorney, have the accountant bill you periodically.

THE REAL ESTATE BROKER

While we can't classify the broker as a member of your team, since he or she works for the seller, it is important to deal with only the best real estate brokers. Select a broker who specializes in the area in which you are interested and who is part of a multiple listing service—your chances of seeing a great variety of suitable homes is much better. Make sure the broker is a member of the National Association of Realtors. That at least ensures a certain level of professionalism. You'll want a licensed broker, not just a salesperson. And don't work with any part-time brokers.

The time to search for a broker is after you have completed your location analysis. At that point you'll be able to look for brokers who have experience and contacts in the neighborhood or town in which you've decided to concentrate your search.

Try to test the broker's ethics during your interview. Ask about homes he doesn't represent. An ethical broker will admit the good points about another broker's listing, at the same time as he or she points out the disadvantages. Brokers aren't legally bound to tell you the truth; therefore it is all the more important that you look for someone who, in your best judgment, seems honest and discreet. Ask if the broker is willing to work with other brokers in the area. If he isn't, go elsewhere. You want someone who is anxious to sell a home, not just protect the size of his or her fee.

Pay careful attention to the questions the broker asks you. The questions asked of you should be nearly as probing and extensive as the self-analysis we performed in drawing up the list of your home-buying priorities.

Test a broker by providing him with your game plan, and then going out on a home visit. If the first home he takes you to comes close to what you're looking for, you've found a good broker. If the house he takes you to indicates that he hasn't paid attention to your needs and wants, then a warning bell should sound and you should begin looking for another broker. Every real estate broker will first take buyers to the home he thinks will be easiest to sell. If the first home doesn't match your vision, it means that the broker either has nothing to fit your needs or has no idea what your needs really are. Inadequate brokers can be a tremendous waste of your time. Discover right away if he will be helping you find your dream home quickly, or will be taking you on trips to nowhere.

THE APPRAISER

While it is not absolutely necessary to have an appraiser on your team, it can be helpful, particularly when you are scouting locations and negotiating. As I shall discuss in Chapter Nine, the only true way to affix a realistic value to a home is to find out what comparable homes have sold for in the recent past. While better brokers may have a firm grasp on comparables, the only sure way to know what a particular home is worth is to get an appraisal, or at least to consult an appraiser. And the time to find an appraiser is as soon as you have finished your location analysis. As with brokers, you'll be looking for an appraiser with experience in your search area. You'll want the appraiser primed and ready to go once you have found a potential purchase.

Select an appraiser who specializes in residential real estate. If you have already selected the financial institution that will be financing your purchase, check with it for the names of appraisers with which it is affiliated, or whom it respects. Your appraiser should be a member of either the American Institute of Real Estate Appraisers, or the Society of Real Estate Appraisers.

During your interview with him, tell the appraiser why you want a writing done on a home. That will determine the fee charged. A simple appraisal report will cost between $150 and $350 and will include pictures of the house and street, a floor plan, and a site map, in addition to the analysis of the value of the home. Appraisers generally charge between $75 and $125 per hour for a consultation. If all you are interested in is the demographics and psychographics of an area, a competent appraiser will generally discuss these with you in under two hours. Some appraisers try to set their fee based on the value of the home they are appraising. This is stupid. The same effort and competence is required to appraise a $100,000 home as a $4 million home.

Ask if the appraiser has done work in the neighborhood you are scouting. Find out how many writings he or she has done in that area in the past year. Watch out for "windshield appraisers" who don't even get out of their car. That's fine for the banker's appraiser, but you want a thorough job. Ask to see a sample of a recent appraisal of a home in the area in question. Tell prospective appraisers you expect them to spring into action at a moment's notice. If they aren't willing, go elsewhere.

THE INSURANCE BROKER

Once you have finished your price negotiation and before the closing, you're going to have to work out your insurance coverage. But insurance costs can play a pivotal role in determining your affordability. Therefore it's important to find an insurance professional to consult *before* you have finished your affordability study.

Deal only with a local insurance broker, as opposed to an insurance agent. Insurance brokers are independent operators who serve their clients' interests, not those of one particular insurance company. He will study your individual needs and search for a policy and an insurance company that offers the best combination of good coverage and low cost. An astute insurance broker will advise you of any improvements that could be made to the property to lower the cost of insurance. Local brokers will be aware of specific area ordinances that will affect your coverage.

Homeowners insurance offers a smorgasbord of options, some crucial, others silly. You'll need a caring, experienced pro to cut through the frills and get down to the essentials of coverage.

Look for an insurance broker who inspires trust and displays a concern for your needs.

Ask the insurance broker about the contacts he or she has with various insurance companies so that you can make a judgment about his or her ability to settle claims. (For more information on homeowners insurance, read Appendix C.)

THE INSPECTOR/ENGINEER

Since inspectors are not involved in the entire purchase process, and aren't called in until the deal is nearing the final stages, it is easy to let a real estate broker sneak a "plant" onto your team. As soon as you've retained an attorney, ask him for the names of three reputable inspectors. Anyone can call himself a home inspector, hang out a shingle and begin practicing as a professional. You'll be looking for an inspector who is a licensed engineer and a member of a professional society, such as the American Society of Home Inspectors. Qualifications such as these ensure that the professional is accountable—he or she has a license or membership that can be revoked for unethical or unprofessional behavior.

Home inspection services are fine for single-family detached home buyers, but if you are shopping for a co-op or condo apartment, it's essential to find a licensed engineer who will be able to evaluate the condition and upkeep of the entire building and all its systems.

Finding an engineer can be difficult. Since few work independently, this is the one member of the team that can be a moonlighter. Ask your lawyer for recommendations.

Reports from engineers and inspectors are meant to be read completely. Don't rush to the last page to see if the home in question has passed or failed "the test." Because you'll be studying the report in depth, you want a pro who will take the time to explain the jargon and terminology it contains. Ask for specimens from both the inspector and engineer. Examine them carefully, checking for thoroughness and an eye for detail, both on interior and exterior structures and systems. If the professional refuses to provide a sample, ask why. Tell the inspector or engineer that the names and address can be blacked out, if privacy is an issue. All you are looking for is thoroughness, not inside dirt on a potential neighbor's home. If a specimen isn't forthcoming, go elsewhere. Look for the most experienced inspecting engineer around. The longer the beard the better. An experienced engineer can often immediately sniff out problems in a home that a neophyte wouldn't discover after even a three-hour examination.

An inspection should take between one and two hours. Ask the inspecting engineer if you can accompany him on the tour of the home. If he objects, ask why.

Don't fall into the trap of praying that the inspector or engineer find nothing wrong. The only pressure you should put on the inspector is to do a thorough job. Many home buyers fall in love with a home and then follow the inspector around trying to convince him that the problems are minor. You are paying for a professional analysis, not a reaffirmation of your own opinions.

Line up an inspector and engineer after you have completed location analysis. You'll want people who have experience in the town or neighborhood in which you are buying (though in a small town you'll have to be careful they're not friends or associates of the seller). Explain that you will need them to move within twenty-four hours of your call to action. If that presents a problem, find someone else.

Inspectors and engineers generally establish a set fee for an investigation, depending on the size and type of home examined. Generally there is little room for negotiation. Fees run between $100 and $300 plus travel. Depending on the real estate and locale, you may have to pay additional fees for a water analysis in addition to urea formaldehyde, radon and asbestos testing as may be required.

THE ARCHITECT

If you are building your own home, an architect is essential. But even if you are buying an existing home, architectural advice can be important in the purchase process. Any renovation work that needs to be done to a home will affect the price you can pay for it. A cottage that must be expanded, or a loft that must be converted, should be examined by an architect before the home is purchased. He or she can tell you if the work you're planning is feasible, and how much it will cost.

Although the choice of an architect is largely a matter of taste, you will want a reputable, competent practitioner. A call to the local chapter of the American Institute of Architects will elicit the names of architects in good standing who do business in your area. The architect is the only team member who needn't be an old, experienced pro. In this field, relative youth, in my experience, can be a plus. We used a young Boston architect to design our home in Martha's Vineyard. His youth brought tremendous energy and originality to the project.

During your interview with the architect, ask to see plans and drawings of homes he has done in the recent past. Discuss your likes and dislikes with the architect. More than any other pro on your team, the architect's personality must be a close match to your own—at least when it comes to matters of taste and style. A good personal rapport is essential. Once you have reached some agreement on the design, have the architect supplement his drawings with a model to help you better visualize your future home. Have the architect prepare specifications and get involved in the bidding process. You want all the contractors bidding on the exact same set of specifications.

In addition to getting the names of the architect's three most recent clients, get the addresses of some local homes designed by the potential team member. Make a point of visiting each of these.

Architects' fees and responsibilities are spelled out in a written contract which will include exactly what services will be provided. Architects may charge on an hourly basis, or establish their fee as a percentage of the construction costs. In addition, architects will charge additional fees if they are responsible for supervising construction work. Set up payments on a periodic basis. Your attorney should be an active part of this contract negotiation.

Your attorney should take an active part in the selection of each subsequent team member. His expertise and experience in the real estate marketplace will help you narrow your search to only the best local professionals.

The key to managing professionals on your team is to walk a fine line between closely supervising their work, and giving them sufficient discretion to do their jobs uninhibited. The best analogy for this tightrope walk is the way you deal with employees and subordinates. You keep track of what they are doing, but leave them enough room to do their jobs as they see fit. But above all else, remember that the professionals work for you.

Many home buyers flinch at the prospect of spending thousands of dollars for the services of professionals. Although it is impossible to generalize about these costs, as they vary from region to region and with the size and complexity of the deal, they will never represent more than a fraction of the purchase price. You will almost certainly pay more in various closing fees and taxes. In fact, fees for professional services are almost always well spent since the benefits, though not tangible, are dollar for dollar as good an investment as the money you will spend in repairing your new home. Both legal and professional services represent relatively inexpensive ways of protecting a very expensive investment. This is not the place to cut corners.

CHAPTER EIGHT

THE
HUNT

To strive, to seek, to find,
and not to yield.
ALFRED, LORD TENNYSON

You've chosen a location. Your team is in place. Now get a good night's sleep, because tomorrow morning the game will be afoot and your senses should be at their sharpest.

While each element of your preparation is invaluable, and every part of the follow-up process is essential, the search is the single most important part of the entire home-buying process. No one else can find the perfect home for you and your family. The wealthy may be able to send out their minions to scour the countryside for a new home. The rest of us have to go it alone. Actually, we're better off; for while the hunt is time consuming, demanding and frustrating, it puts us in control of our own destinies. Our parents were right: Anything worth possessing is worth pursuing. And while it may be intimidating at first, the analysis of location is an indispensible learning experience. Each day you spend scouring a community brings you closer to expert status. You'll find that after a week of searching a town you'll not only be knowledgeable about the area but you'll also have become an educated home consumer, adept at differentiating the truth from the propaganda. If you are under a time deadline, location analysis can be doubly difficult. All I can tell you is that it's better to buy the right home a little late, than the wrong home on time.

Our pursuit can follow three routes: the newspaper, real estate brokers and pounding the pavement searching out "for sale" signs. In the beginning, eliminate the latter route. We've all heard stories of people who stumbled onto their dream house, walked in the door, made an offer and shook hands—all within an hour. But these tales are mostly folklore held over from an earlier, less complicated America.

Today, no home worth owning is passing time on the market unadvertised except for the hand-lettered sign on the front lawn. Those homemade signs carry an added message for the astute buyer: Beware! You'll be dealing with inept sellers who will in all likelihood have no idea about the market value of their homes or the intricacies of the selling process. Sure, a bargain may lie behind that front door. But finding out isn't worth the trouble. The real estate market has evolved into its present structure for a host of reasons, primary among them being efficiency.

And don't fall victim to the mistaken belief that a home sold without a broker will save you money. The brokerage commission of 6 percent has become such a fixture on the American real estate scene that it has worked its way into the market value figure. Just as you may believe that you will be able to cut the price 6 percent by avoiding a broker, the home owner thinks he or she can boost the price 6 percent. There is no price disadvantage to buying through a broker, and in fact, there are advantages for the buyer. Brokers, at least the good ones, will help you negotiate price and offer valuable information on both the community and the seller.

Instead of setting out on the search blindly, pick up the major newspaper covering your selected location. You're looking for leads on area brokers and ideas on prices. The Sunday editions of papers are always the most promising for real estate ads. But don't wait for Sunday morning. Make it your business to get a jump on the market by picking up the paper Saturday or even Friday night. If you've been nice to the paperboy at Christmas, you may be able to wheedle the Sunday real estate section (which is almost always a preprinted insert) out of him long before the bulk of the paper arrives. If you have to beg the newsstand owner, do it. Before hitting the sack, scour the ads, and jot down the phone numbers of promising properties. When the sun comes up Sunday morning you'll be making calls while the less prepared buyer will be just opening the real estate section.

This early bird technique works just as well for new homes as old homes. Developers often open up new projects at a low price, gauging by the response the accurate price level. By late Sunday afternoon, prices may have gone up. Being at the starting line early can save you dollars as well as time and trouble.

Real estate ads are written to attract and dazzle you. Only the most foolish homeowner writes his or her own real estate ad. Instead, brokers, or professional ad writers in the classified departments of newspapers, come up with eye-catching, dream-inspiring jargon that make real estate ads pop off the page. These experts will encourage sellers to include words and phrases that work. Don't fall for catchy words and phrases like "cozy" or "handyman's special"; these are euphemisms for small and dilapidated. Phrases like "light and airy" and "bright and sunny" are subjective. Instead, pay attention only to the facts. How many bedrooms and bathrooms are there? What is the exact location? What size is the lot? How many of your priorities and needs are answered in the ad?

Don't visit a listing without first calling the seller or broker. On the phone, be direct. If a broker answers the phone, ask for all the pertinent details in order to discover right away if the home fits your goals. We've devoted a great deal of time and soul-searching to come up with these goals. Don't let a persuasive broker or seller convince you that even though it is only a two-bedroom home, it's worth seeing. There are thousands of homes on the market, and hundreds more being added each day. Now isn't the time to compromise. And don't let a broker talk you into meeting him at the home in question. Set up an appointment at the broker's office.

Once at his office, ask for a photo of the home advertised. Get the details on the block or neighborhood. While your location analysis has given you a firm grounding in the general area, a good broker will help in finding out about individual blocks' or buildings' character. Ask about the neighborhood school. Find out about shopping. Discover all you can about the particular home's location before setting out to see it. If the broker hasn't seen the home in question yet, don't bother taking a tour with him. How can he know if it fits your goals if he hasn't been there? You'll be providing the broker with a more detailed picture of your needs and wants than the average buyer. He should be able to weed through his listings and prequalify various homes for you. That is one of the true benefits of working through a broker. While the advertised home may not fit your needs, a good broker will be able to pull out a number of other listings that may more accurately match your goals.

A close friend and former associate of mine has gone on to become a highly successful real estate broker. She realized early on that the more clients she saw, the more opportunities she would have to close a sale. Her technique has been polished and honed to the point where today she can be all things to all people. By being understanding and appearing to appreciate a buyer's needs completely, she can convince them she knows what is best for them. She would set a date to show them four or five homes, each of which was "perfect for them." Many times she could actually intimidate buyers into accepting her judgments and tastes. She would state that these homes were the only ones available for the buyer— thus limiting their universe to her listings. By adopting the role of the buyers' caring, intelligent Auntie Mame, she could often blast them out of their mind-set into adopting one of her choosing. The moral of the story: Make sure that every broker you deal with actually understands your needs and wants. Don't let them "yes" you into submission, or intimidate you into accepting their view of what is good and what isn't.

If the seller answers the phone listed in the ad, try to find out at least three-quarters of the information that a broker would provide. Remember, though, that the seller will be less likely to report honestly on the character of both the home and the neighborhood. Try to phrase your questions specifically to elicit objective rather than subjective answers. Ask for square footage rather than whether the home is large or small. Find out how many bedrooms there are, not how many occupants there are. Ask if the house or apartment has a new kitchen, not if the kitchen is "nice." Ask if you can sit and eat in the kitchen, or if you can fit a sofa bed in the den, to gauge room sizes.

It is probably a good idea to avoid starting your search with homes "for sale by owner." Most will be overpriced since the seller isn't aware of the true market value of his or her property, and you won't yet have the experience in the area to talk them down. Save these properties for later in the search when you've become an old pro and are more confident in your value judgments. "For sale" signs are, more often than not, invitations for brokers. I've even heard of home owners who put up such signs to scare the neighbors, to get an idea of the value of their home or even to threaten a spouse.

In the early stages of the search, beware of open houses at model homes in new developments. You are looking to buy a home today, not six months from now. Model homes and apartments are enticing and alluring, not unlike those beautiful models that tout other products. As a newcomer to the search, you won't have the experience to judge if a new development is overpriced for the area. Besides, you don't want to fall in love with a fully furnished and finished dream that represents only what your unit will look like five years, or $50,000 from now.

These models can help you gauge the relative values of a new home versus an old home in the area where you have centered your search, but only after you have an idea of what else is out there. And models can help you develop ideas for decorating and furnishing your own home. Use them as you would an article or advertisement in a home magazine—for dreaming, not for buying.

Once you have set up an appointment with a broker, arrive prepared to judge not only the homes, but the broker. Arrive with your spouse or alone. Do not bring children or pets with you. Both will be cranky, bored and eager for your attention—attention that will be better spent on the home. Check into the broker's knowledge of the community. What part of town do they live in? And how long have they lived there? If they are from out of town, go elsewhere. A good broker will have accurate information not only on the home itself, but on the town government, stores, schools, garbage collection and recreation. Ask how long the broker has been in business. A newcomer isn't for you. Experience is a must. If he is a part-timer, walk away. You'll be living in your home full-time, and you want someone who takes his business seriously.

Judge the competence of brokers by the questions they ask you. Do they "qualify" your affordability by asking questions to confirm that you can handle the price range you've cited? While you shouldn't let them determine your affordability, their questioning indicates a certain degree of professionalism. If you must, tailor the information you give them about your financial history so that your ability to buy isn't a question in their mind. Do they ask you specific questions about your goals? Have they seen the properties in question? Do they know local lawyers and bankers? Get as much information as you possibly can. Ask for street maps and any printed information on the community. A good broker will have pamphlets from organizations like the League of Women Voters, the library, the recreation department, the council on the arts and others. Ask for a local train or bus schedule and prices for tickets.

Look at the multiple listings for the area. An ethical broker will provide you with a complete listing of properties for sale that includes price, details on size and pictures. Don't be afraid to ask for the broker's opinion on a listing. He should have seen almost every available property within reason. Decor, size, style, condition, floor plan and siting should all be on the tip of a broker's tongue. If he says he hasn't seen the home and invites you to go along with him for a first look, turn him down. A good broker will check listings out on his own, prequalifying them for you so as not to waste your time. He will offer to look into a listing for you, and only take you to homes he has already scouted.

Ask for comparables—the selling prices of homes similar to the one you are about to see. The more recent the comparables, and the closer they are to the home in question, the more professional the broker.

The best way to judge a broker is by going on one visit with him. Does the home you are being shown match up with the needs, wants and price you have discussed with the broker? If not, leave, and don't come back. You don't have the time to waste with an uneducated, incompetent broker.

An ethical broker will tell you about potential problems before you discover them. Anything obvious enough for you to see right away should be addressed by the broker before you even lay eyes on the place. A broker who tries to dissuade you from using other brokers, or looking at other homes, is unethical as well as incompetent. If he tells you how bad other brokers are, or notes that the next town over is going to seed, he isn't the broker for you. Does he let the home sell itself, pointing out only those advantages that aren't readily apparent, or does he hit you over the head with a hard sell? Good brokers will let you take your time and examine the home. (And after finishing this chapter we are going to be experts at conducting this first tour.) If a broker pressures you by saying that there is someone else ready to buy the home, tell him you hope that that other family will be happy here, and then leave. There's no reason for a broker to apply pressure this early on, unless he is desperate. Remember that, no matter how ethical a broker is, he will always pass on anything you say to the seller. But knowledge of this duplicity can turn a potential problem into a tool, as I will demonstrate in Chapter Nine, where we consider negotiation.

I learned this the hard way. I was bidding on a wonderful co-op apartment for a client of mine. I foolishly took the broker into my confidence and said that while the price wasn't too bad, I was going to try to get it down a bit for my client. After all, I had worked with the broker four or five other times. I had him submit a lowball bid and tried negotiating with the seller. I got nowhere, and finally, my client paid the price. Later I learned that the broker had advised the seller that we thought the original price was fair and that they should avoid negotiating until we came up to the asking price.

Always let the broker do the driving. He is on the job, you are not. In addition, he will probably know the community better than you do. While he is driving to and from homes, you can take notes, ask questions about the stores you pass, gauge the traffic and just observe. If you are accompanied by a spouse or friend, save your private conversations for your ride home from the broker's office. Later on, when we begin negotiating price, we'll learn how, when and what information to provide the broker. For now, hold all your cards close to the vest.

Dress conservatively and appropriately, in style for the season and region—in neat, clean clothing. Don't wear your bathing suit, halter top, or cut-off jeans. This is serious business, and you want all involved, including the seller, to know that you are a serious buyer.

Don't see more than five homes in one day. Any more and you will begin to confuse them. You'll find that when you sit down at the end of the day you won't remember whether it was the Cape Cod on Maple Street or the colonial on Elm that had the skylight in the kitchen. Have the agent schedule visits to five houses that are near one another. You want to spend your time looking at homes, not sitting in traffic, or crisscrossing town. Start early enough so that every home will be seen in bright, clear daylight. Sellers will be camouflaging any faults. You don't need to help them in their efforts.

Never express extremely positive opinions on any property you see with a broker. Be calm, confident and professional. You are going to be the expert home shopper, comparing, taking notes and inspecting each site as if it were a car in the dealer's showroom.

For the first visit to a home you will bring with you a reconnaissance kit: a shoulder bag or briefcase with an instant camera and film; a small tape recorder; a tape measure; a compass; pens and pencils; a notepad; a set of binoculars; a tennis ball (to check for level floors); and your list of needs, wants and priorities.

This first tour of the site should be short—no more than thirty minutes. But in this amount of time you will be able to decide if the home fits in with your needs and wants, and represents a sound investment.

On the way to your first stop, carefully study the immediate area around the home. Are there factories nearby? What about train tracks and highways? How far away are stores and schools? What do other homes on the block look like? Conduct another location analysis during the drive, reacquainting yourself with the general area, and noting any specifics about the block or neighborhood. If you see a major factory complex nearby, or—God forbid—a garbage dump or sewage plant, don't even get out of the car. Have the broker turn around and take you back to his office. The slightest hint of possible environmental pollution should sound a siren in your head. Not only will environmental problems cut into resale values, they could kill you. Remember the old real estate axiom: Nearby vacant lots owned by someone else are time bombs.

Enroute to the home ask the broker: how long it has been on the market; approximately when it was built and when any extensions were done; if the brokerage firm helped set the price; what type of person the seller is; why the home is being sold; and what offers, if any, have been rejected. This information starts you off with a technicolor view of the economics of the property, rather than the black-and-white picture the broker will be projecting. Rather than color the home with propaganda, get the broker to provide economic information that can help you make an enlightened judgment.

With your list of needs and wants in hand, take a good first look at the house. In the back of your mind throw the switch that separates your heart from your head and proceed from this point on as an emotionally detached observer of details. You should be coldly rational as you examine the scene. When you get home you can temper your logic with emotion, but for the time being, leave feelings out of it.

Assuming that the broker has done his or her job, the home will have the correct number of bedrooms and bathrooms, be located in the type of neighborhood you want, and be of the proper type and style. If so, start by examining the exterior. Whether single-family detached or multifamily, all homes share certain elements. You'll want to examine the yard and landscaping, the external wall coverings, any indoor/outdoor spaces, the roof, the garage (and any other additional structures) and the foundation. Using the binoculars, scan the roof for any obvious signs of trouble such as sags or dips.

Is the lawn well cared for or in need of reseeding? Does it appear that the trees, bushes and shrubs have been regularly maintained? Have branches been pruned away from windows, power/telephone lines and walls? Are fences or sheds in good repair or falling apart? Is the driveway paved? What about the sidewalks and walkways around the home? Are there cracks or sections missing? Are there lights around the home? How about streetlights? Take photos of the front, rear and side landscaping, from the house and from the street. Make note of any landscaping problems that will need attention.

What are the views surrounding the home? In certain areas of the country, particularly large urban areas, views of water, greenery and mountains can add 20 to 30 percent to the price of a home. But don't assume that, because a house has a picture window, it has a great view—it might overlook nothing more than a road. And don't take anyone's word about "obscured views."

While shopping for my home on Martha's Vineyard, a

broker described to me the wonderful view that would materialize once a group of trees was chopped down. I handed the broker—a man younger than myself—my binoculars and asked him to climb one of the trees and describe the view. He returned red-faced. The picturesque vista he described would never appear no matter how many trees I cut down.

The views from apartments are often more important than those from single-family home, since apartments are by their very nature smaller and more confining. Other important exterior features to scrutinize when examining an apartment are the downstairs lobby, hallways, laundry rooms, trash disposal areas, elevator interiors and basement facilities. The condition of these common areas in a building is indicative of the care and concern of the co-op board or the condo managing agent. Talk to the doorman, if there is one. Not only will his attitude go a long way in disclosing the quality of management in the building, but he might also be the source of further intelligence and information. Ask him, the broker or other residents about recent sales. Find out how good the superintendent is.

Look at the grading of the property and the surrounding areas. Is the home for sale at the bottom of a hill or glen, or alongside a hill? Any site that doesn't allow water to drain off away from it, is dangerous. If the home looks like it spends a lot of time underwater, leave before you even get close enough to read the number on the house.

What are the exterior walls constructed of and covered with: masonry, clapboard, wooden shingles, aluminum siding . . . asbestos shingles? Whatever the wall covering, what condition is it in? Do shingles need to be replaced? Are there cracks in the siding? Is there any evidence of dry rot or decay, such as crumbling windowsills or doorjambs? Are corners and joints caulked, and if so, in what condition is the caulking? Do you notice any signs of water damage or blistering paint? Will the exterior walls need to be painted or repaired immediately? If you notice zigzag cracking in the masonry of walls, or if there are signs of uneven settling, go no further. A few hairline cracks in masonry are to be expected in an older home, however, and should not discourage further searching. Any signs that that type of damage has recently been covered up should set off alarms in your head. Again, take photos of all sides of the home. If anything looks suspicious, take a close up shot.

Does the home have any indoor/outdoor areas, such as decks, porches or patios? What condition are they in? Do they appear to be sound, or in need of repair? Do they fit in with the style and design of the home, or look like a weekend project? A poorly built, unmaintained wooden structure, such as a deck, that has begun to rot or decay, can spread its ailment to the rest of the home. If the structure isn't sound, it could be placing stress on the rest of the home. Far from being an amenity, a poorly maintained, inadequate deck or porch can be a curse.

Think in terms of security. How close are the neighbors? Can rear windows be reached from the ground? Can thieves attempt entry without being seen from the street? Do locks on doors and accessible windows work? Is there a burglar alarm system? How does it operate? Can it be connected to a central station or the police department? Are there several ways to leave the home in case of fire? Are there fire escapes? What about smoke alarms? How about accessibility for the handicapped or elderly?

Take a look at the roof. On this first visit we aren't going to climb a rickety ladder and take life in hand to examine, firsthand, the roof of a prospective home. Instead, just make some observations from the ground with your binoculars. What material is used on the roof: slate or tile, wood or asphalt shingles? What type of roof is it: flat or pitched? Does it appear to be in good condition? Are there any noticeable gaps in the roofing material? What about the flashing? Can you see any areas that may have been patched recently? Examine the chimney. Is the brick or stone in good shape? How about the mortar? Check the leaders and gutters. Are there enough downspouts? Are there any water stains visible? Check the ground near the downspouts for signs of flooding. Does it appear that the gutters have been cleaned recently? Are there any gaps in the drainage system? Check for dips in the roofline that could indicate a structural problem. If the house looks like Dorothy's after landing in Oz, don't waste any more time on it.

Make note of, and photograph, any outbuildings such as garages or sheds. Check them for the same structural problems as the main buildings. If they are in poor condition, chances are you'll find problems in the main house as well. Outbuilding condition is a good indicator of the owner's general maintenance standards. If the main house doesn't provide you with enough storage for your needs, don't count on an outbuilding or garage to make up the difference.

While walking around the building, examine the foundation. Look for signs of uneven settling, such as cracks and gaps between foundation and walls. If there is the slightest sign of foundation problems, leave. You're not going to build your life on an unreliable base.

Note what types, and how many, windows are on each side of the house. Are there storm or screen windows? How about picture windows and skylights? Are the window frames in good shape or are there signs of rot? Make sure that all the windowpanes are in place. Any cracked glass indicates that the owner's approach to maintenance is lackadaisical.

Take out your compass and sketch the layout of the house on the lot, placing windows in their proper areas. Note exposures for each side of the home, and check what types of landscaping are near or around the various exposures. Southern exposures should be protected by deciduous trees. In layman's terms, that means no evergreens. In the winter (when deciduous trees have no leaves) the warm southern sun should be let into the house, while in summer (when those same trees are in full leaf) it should be blocked to keep the house cool. Northern exposures should have evergreen trees nearby, offering protection from the sun in the summer and the wind in the winter. Check to see which rooms will receive morning light, which afternoon light and which will be forever dark.

At each step in your exterior examination, check for any sign of insect infestation. You may not be an entomologist, and we can't make you one, but keep your eyes open for undue concentrations of insects at the joints between foundation and siding, roof and wall, window and wall. If you see a long line of insects marching their way into the house, march yourself in the opposite direction.

Make an overall judgement on the style of the house. Does it fit in with the rest of the neighborhood? Very few American homes are actually designed by architects. Most are drawn up and constructed by builders and general contractors who are businessmen, not artists. The key aesthetic issue is: Does your home fit in with its neighbors? Remember, one day we are going to be reselling this home. Tastes may change from year to year, but as long as a home is true to its environment, it will always remain in style.

If the home passes your exterior tests, which should only have taken 15 minutes to complete, take the big step and cross the threshold.

Don't be overly concerned with the doors to the home. Instead, concentrate on the entranceway. Good entries will have wide walks or steps, an adequate shelter from the elements, and be in keeping with the rest of the home's style.

Before examining specific rooms in the house or apartment, think about the flow of rooms and the traffic patterns people will take through them. Make notes using your tape recorder as you move from room to room, and sketch out a floor plan if possible. Indicate doors and windows. Are there any rooms that can only be entered through another room? In the case of the kitchen, that's okay. But a bedroom which can be entered only through another bedroom is a problem not only for everyday living, but for resale as well. How does one go from the living area (family room, living room and kitchen) to the bathroom? When you come home from the store with a bundle of groceries, how far will you have to walk to get to the kitchen? Are there any stairs between the driveway or entrance and the kitchen? How will guests enter the home? Is there a formal entryway which allows easy access to the living room or dining room? Is there a lavatory nearby for guests, or will they have to use a bathroom in a bedroom? Is there access from the kitchen to the yard, deck or patio? How about closets? Is there a coat closet near the front door? A linen closet near the bedrooms? Will you have a place to store mops, brooms and cleaning supplies near the kitchen? Do any of the halls or foyers appear long and dark? The actual length and lighting of halls, or rooms for that matter, isn't as important as their apparent size or brightness. Don't worry about details at this point. Instead, look for objectionable traffic patterns.

Make careful note of walls, floors and ceilings throughout the house. Do the floors creak or appear uneven? Here's where the tennis ball comes in. If you sense that the flooring is uneven, take the tennis ball and place it carefully on the floor. If this is a fairly new house and it starts to roll, you've got problems. You should roll just as fast for the front door, since uneven flooring is usually a sign of extensive structural problems. In an old house a certain amount of settling inevitably takes place. As long as the tennis ball doesn't move too quickly or too far, the home should be fine. Are the walls, whatever they are covered with—wallpaper, panelling, paint, tile—in good shape? Do you see any holes or cracks? Check the moldings between floors and walls and between walls and ceilings. Are any missing? Do there appear to be problems with the joints? Check the ceiling. Is there any sign of water damage? If there is, glance down at the floor in the same spot. There's probably damage there as well. As you enter each room, take out your tape measure and determine its approximate size. If the broker offers to help, make sure you hold the "smart end"—don't rely on him to read off the measurement.

The first rooms to check, since they are the most expensive to repair or renovate, are the kitchen and bathrooms.

Is there room to eat in the kitchen? How much counter space is there? Are the major work areas—sink, refrigerator, stove/oven—set up in a triangle relationship to each other? Is there a window over the sink? What about cabinet space? Will you be able to store all your foodstuffs, cookware, dinnerware and utensils? Are the built-in appliances and the refrigerator in good working order? If the kitchen needs to be redone, and your budget doesn't allow for it, find another home.

Adequate bathroom facilities are essential. Never assume that you can add another bathroom to bring the home up to your goals. The cost is often prohibitive, and it may in fact prove impossible. All bathrooms should have either windows or ventilation systems. Check to see if bathrooms have walk-in showers or bath/shower combinations. Test the water pressure in each shower and sink. Turn on each faucet in the bathroom and see if the flow of water is even. How does flushing the toilet effect water pressure? Are there any electrical outlets in the bathroom? How about the condition of tiles and walls? Is there grout missing? Inspect the fixtures. Is the porcelain cracked or pitted? Check the drainage in sinks, showers and tubs. Drop a wad of toilet paper in the bowl and observe how quickly the tank flushes. If the bathrooms aren't up to your standards, walk away. It is an extremely expensive proposition to remodel, let alone add a new bathroom, particularly after stretching to buy a home.

While in the kitchen and bathrooms, look for the laundry facilities. A washer/dryer set up in the basement or kitchen isn't as attractive as in a separate room off the kitchen, but as long as there are adequate laundry facilities in the home, don't worry.

Pay careful attention to closets. There should be at least one closet in each bedroom, a front hall closet for guests' coats, a linen closet near the bedrooms for sheets and towels, and a utility closet near the kitchen for brooms and cleaning supplies. The more closets the better. Don't be overly concerned with closet interiors. For a minimal investment, a closet can be redone. But make sure to open each and every closet door. If one is locked, ask why.

Examine each bedroom carefully. How much light is coming into the room? (Here's a good time to walk around shutting off electric lights to check the natural light that comes into the home.) How close is each bedroom to a bathroom? If the bedrooms are in attic areas, have dormers been added to bring in additional light? Is there a high enough ceiling to allow some freedom of movement? Will each bedroom be large enough for its probable occupant?

In bedrooms, and, in fact, in every room, watch out for skillfully placed mirrors which could be used to make dinky hallways appear grand and widen narrow rooms. Lift up rugs to check the floor underneath. Sometimes they can be used to camouflage damage. Any furniture or fixture that appears out of the ordinary could very well be there to obscure a problem.

Is there a family room or den in the home? How large is it?

If the room is going to combine entertainment, informal dining and family activities, it will have to be large enough to hold all the necessary furniture. How much light is there in the room? Does it give access to outdoor areas?

How large is the formal living room? Will it be large enough to entertain guests? If there is no family room or den, the living room will have to house informal as well as formal gatherings. If there is a family room, you can probably get by with a smaller living room.

Is there a formal dining room, or a dining area? Does the room have access to both the kitchen and living rooms? Is it large enough to accommodate at least six diners?

Is there an attic or basement in the house? How do you enter each? Are there permanent attic stairs, or pull-down stairs in the hallway? Is access limited to a hatch in a closet? Can the basement be entered without going outside? Does the basement show signs of water damage? Does it smell of mildew? How much lighting is provided? If there is no basement, where are the furnace and water heater located? Utility rooms should be large enough for repairs to be made, but shouldn't steal space from the rest of the house.

Basements are often the scene of the worse propaganda ploys and camouflage tactics. One of my homes had a terrible flooding problem. Each time it rained I was left with two or three inches of water sitting on the basement floor. When it came time to sell, I had the basement painted to cover up the water damage, installed a dehumidifier to take out the mildew odor, and made it my business to show the home only on sunny days.

Electrical service, particularly in older homes and apartments, can be a source of trouble. Check to see how much voltage is coming into the home or apartment. Are the outlets modern or old-fashioned? If they accept three-prong grounded plugs, you are in good shape. If lots of extension cords are in use, assume that you'll have to add service after moving in. While in the basement or garage, check the fuse box. If fuses rather than circuit breakers are installed, the service hasn't been changed since the original construction. Any sign of fuses, covered with silver foil, or pennies used to replace fuses and you can be sure you're standing in a fire hazard. Modern circuit breaker panels are a plus, particularly if they are labeled and allow for more lines to be added.

The interior tour should only take fifteen minutes, but after this reconnaissance you will at least be able to determine whether the home is worth a second look. And you will be back if the home holds out hope. Before making an offer on any home, visit it twice. The first visit may have seemed exhaustive, but it actually is only intended to search out obvious and substantial problems, and to see if the home fits your list of needs, wants and goals. Your return trip will let you examine the house's operating systems more closely, as well as probe beneath the home's skin. The first visit is merely to take the pulse. The second is by way of a thorough checkup.

The return trip to the home should be made by appointment, since you will spend at least an hour inspecting the property. This time, dress a bit more informally, since you will be doing some dirty work. Add to your shoulder bag a screwdriver, flashlight and night-light. And bring along a stepladder.

Work your way through the house once more, except this time, check each electrical outlet with the night-light, noting any that do not work. See if there is any room without sufficient electrical outlets—at least two on opposing walls are mandatory. Does the home have 200, 150, 100 or 60 amp service? Usually, any service lower than 200 will have to be updated. How many 15 amp and 20 amp circuits are there in the home? Are there enough heavier lines (30 amp or more) for major appliances such as air conditioners, large freezers or clothes dryers? Check the wiring leading into the breaker or fuse box. Is it insulated with cloth or plastic?

After reexamining the electrical system, check out the heating and air conditioning systems. What type of boiler system is in the house: gravity hot water, forced hot water or steam? A forced hot water boiler will have a circulating pump. A steam system will have single pipe radiators throughout the home. Is the furnace gravity hot air or forced hot air? Gravity hot air systems have vents in the side of the furnace. What type of energy is used to heat the home: gas, oil, electricity, a combination or another? Check the air conditioning system of the home by turning all the units on. Turn on the heating system by boosting the thermostat up as high as possible. Now walk throughout the house checking first the air conditioning vents, then the heating devices. Make note of any that doesn't work. Make sure there is sufficient insulation around the heating and cooling equipment. Check that there is an emergency shutoff switch and valve near the furnace and water heater. Examine carefully each part of the heating and cooling system for corrosion. Replacement of segments of the system can be expensive, but unless the system looks unsalvageable, these problems should not deter you from purchasing the home.

The next area to examine is the plumbing and water system. What is the source of the home's water: municipal or a well? Are shutoff valves provided in each room, or in one central location? Is there a separate hot water heater, or is it connected to the home's heating system? What are the pipes made of: copper, galvanized steel, brass or plastic? Are the pipes new, or do they leak and appear in need of replacement? Do you notice any stains from water damage? Unless there are noticeable problems with the plumbing system, leave the final determination of its fitness to your expert inspector.

Whether the home is in a cold or warm climate, insulation is important. Make sure that there are storm windows provided if you are in a northern climate. In addition, check each outside wall of the home for insulation. Instead of trusting the home owner or broker to divulge the insulation value of the house, unscrew an electrical face plate from each exterior wall. Look alongside the electrical junction box for insulation. Check the caulking and weatherproofing around windows and doors. Get out your flashlight and venture into the utility areas of the home. If there is a crawl space or basement beneath a living area, check for insulation on the ceiling. Look for a ventilation system. Measure the thickness of the insulation present. Take the stepladder and climb up to the attic to check for insulation on both the floor and the roof. Again, measure the insulation and check for a venting system to cut down on heat buildup. The thicker the insulation the higher the insulating quality, known as R value. Look around heating and cooling ducts throughout the home for insulation materials. Lack of insulation can be a drawback to a home, but shouldn't necessarily keep you from making an offer. Check for vent openings under the eaves and in the peak of the roof. Make sure there is clearance between any attic insulation and the roof itself. If these areas aren't kept open for air flow, they will rot quickly.

Before finishing your second inspection tour, try to find out, either from the broker or the seller, the age of the home, and what systems and appliances have been replaced. Each part of a home has a life expectancy, and you can expect to replace various items as they reach the end of their useful lives. By finding out the ages of the systems in the home, as well as the home itself, you can estimate your future costs and expenses. Deferred maintenance is one of the major traps to look out for. Delaying that paint job doesn't really save money. When it finally *has* to be done, it will cost more because it hasn't been kept up. Here is a general guide to the lifespan of a home's various components:

After the first five years of a home's life you can expect to replace or repair: exterior paint on wood or brick; interior paint on walls, trim and doors; wallpaper; fluorescent lightbulbs; and gravel walks.

During years five through ten homeowners should be prepared to shell out money for the following: reglazing the windows; screen doors; carpeting; drapes; splash blocks; asphalt driveways; and possibly a host of new appliances such as washers, dryers, garage door openers, humidifiers, garbage disposals and dishwashers.

In years ten through fifteen some serious maintenance problems may crop up. At this point, problems may be found in: precast decks and porches; tar/gravel roofs; storm doors; interior doors; electric roof fans; exterior wooden trim; painted aluminum on the exterior of the house; luminous ceilings; vinyl flooring; mirrors; kitchen and bathroom exhaust fans; doorbells and chimes; gas water heaters; toilet seats; air conditioning compressors; window blinds; towel bars; soap grabs; sprinkler systems and concrete walks.

As the home reaches twenty, expect to make substantial

investments in: asphalt shingles; kitchen cabinets; bathroom vanities; countertops; medicine cabinets; tub enclosures; shower doors; electric ranges and ovens; vent hoods; commodes; steel and china sinks; flush valves; well and septic systems; and refrigerators.

In years twenty through thirty homeowners will have to be prepared for expenses in: new circuit breakers; built-up asphalt roofs; masonry fireplaces; garage doors; wood and metal shutters; electric fixtures; ceiling and baseboard heating fixtures; and fences and screens.

Between years thirty and fifty investments will have to be made in: outside gravel; new circuit breaker panels; galvanized iron or plastic pipes; heating and ventilation ducts; wood, tile and asbestos roofs; sliding and folding doors; casement, double hung and jalousie windows; interior stairways; drywall; interior wood trim; and flagstone floors. As the home nears fifty years old all remaining original systems will have to be replaced.

After determining the age of the home, pay particular attention during your second visit inspection to the age of those systems which are, according to statistics, about to end their useful lives. You need to know how much money you'll be likely to spend in the first year or so. And recognizing a major component in need of replacement will give you important ammunition during the negotiation.

Don't let sellers and brokers lead you to believe that amenities—hot tubs, whirlpools, bidets, floor-to-ceiling ceramic tile, fireplaces, skylights and wet bars—are being thrown in. Their cost was almost certainly added into the asking price of a home. While the extras may add spice to the home, they aren't important in the context of setting your goals. You can always add amenities later on.

During your two tours of the home keep in mind that you are buying not only shelter but an investment. Unless you intend to spend the rest of your life in this particular home, you will find yourself on the other side of the transaction someday soon. Bear in mind that home buyers are looking not for an unusual home, but one that fits a set of standard desires and wants. Home hunters are today looking for: an open floor plan; larger kitchens than in the past; high quality workmanship and materials; amenities in exchange for size; energy efficiency; and a room, such as a den or family room, for informal entertaining.

Keep in mind that you can't expect to take the place of an experienced professional inspector. In fact, I will discuss dealing with an engineer/inspector later, in Chapter Ten. But inspectors deal only with the most obvious and major parts of a home. Before spending $200 to $300 for a professional inspector's visit, take the time to look on your own for potential problems. You don't need an inspector to tell you that a flooded basement or sinking foundation isn't good. Take charge. Be an informed and educated home shopper. The more carefully you inspect the home yourself, the more confidence you will have when it comes time to negotiate. Any problems you discover now can help you cut down the seller's price during the negotiation. And if major problems are uncovered, you can avoid wasting time and money.

If after two trips you haven't found any serious problems, and you are sure that your needs and wants are met by the home, it's time to make an offer and begin the negotiating process.

CHAPTER NINE

THE
NEGOTIATION

Audentes fortuna juvat.
(Fortune favors the bold.)
VIRGIL

Americans approach negotiation as if it were some kind of arcane ritual. The classic image of the negotiating process involves two middle-aged men in slightly rumpled suits hammering away at each other and accentuating their points by gesticulating wildly with cigars. We tend to think of negotiation as a vaguely mysterious process, invariably taking place behind closed doors. Perhaps these misconceptions account for the popularity of scores of books promising to tell all about the crafty tricks of "power negotiating," or the gimmicks promised by the "needs theory."

In fact, most of us will never find ourselves in the stereotypical smoke-filled room. Our negotiations are more likely to take place in an employer's office, a car salesman's showroom, or—in the case of the real estate negotiation—seated around a kitchen table, or perhaps over the telephone. And all those neat stratagems for power negotiating don't help when the opponent happens to be an emotional home owner who refuses to deal with you directly, referring you instead to a real estate broker.

Rather than gimmicks and shortcuts, the techniques of real estate negotiation are simple and straightforward—even old fashioned and traditional. The only thing new about negotiation is the jargon.

Don't misunderstand. The negotiation is serious business. This purchase involves hundreds of thousands of dollars. Even if you negotiate only a 10 or 15 percent reduction in the asking price, that could involve a room full of furniture, a new car, a renovated nursery or a new landscaping job. But just because the stakes are high doesn't mean you need a bagful of tricks and gimmicks to succeed in the real estate negotiation. Preparation, objectivity and common sense are your most effective guides.

The most important part of the negotiation actually takes place long before you make your first offer on the home. By the time you get down to business, you will have prepared for the negotiation with all the deliberation and dedication that Eisenhower brought to the Normandy invasion. You'll start by gathering all the intelligence you can about the seller's needs and wants: Is he or she really prepared to sell? Why is the home being sold? Is the seller under any time pressure? By thus interrogating the broker, you'll learn the home's history—how long it has been on the market, what other offers have been made, how many people have seen the home and not made offers. Having completed your location and site analyses (Chapters Seven and Eight), you'll know all the details and peculiarities of the home and its location. You will have unearthed the facts about the following: the town or neighborhood's political and economic character; the block's place in the community mosaic; the home's physical condition; and the area's demographics and psychographics. But by far the most essential preparation of all involves the locating and nailing down of your own priorities.

You're not looking for a steal. Part of being an astute home buyer is realizing that a home has a fair market value. I've read everything written about negotiation. I've learned—and occasionally used—all of those cute tricks that the experts advise. But after thirty-five years of personal involvement in the real estate business—negotiating as a buyer and a seller, acting as an attorney for both sides and even acting as a broker—I've discovered that the best negotiations are those that treat both sides fairly. You are in the negotiation to make a deal, not to win. Don't look to beat anyone. If you don't aim at winning, you probably won't open yourself up to losing.

My years of negotiating have taught me that the overriding motivation on both sides is to avoid losing face, and that the overriding emotion for both buyer and seller is fear. Almost everyone is afraid of being embarrassed—of settling for too low an offer, for example, or paying too high a price. The single best way to transcend this fear is to approach the process honestly and fairly, seeking a deal that will satisfy both parties' needs. Your weapon is the knowledge you've gathered, and your armor is the air of truth and logic you bring to the process. Let's call our strategy "fair negotiation."

It's up to you to set the proper tone, because sellers are under more stress than buyers. They have only one product on the market. And if they truly want to sell, they are often under financial and time constraints—for example, they may already have selected another home which they must close on quickly. Buyers are really much better off than sellers, but few home shoppers realize this. There is no single perfect home that you were "meant" to buy. If this deal doesn't work, another will. For sellers, each offer may be the last.

If you've read and absorbed all of the information contained in the preceding chapters you should know that homes have a market value based on their location and physical condition. Homes in the same neighborhood, or apartments in the same building, may vary in price by 10 to 15 percent—due to where they fit in the neighborhood or building's overall environment. The value of a home isn't what you are willing to pay, or what the seller is willing to accept. Instead, it is what the market dictates. As the buyer, it's easy for you to come to terms with this. The seller, on the other hand, brings a lot of emotional baggage to the transaction. The home is more than four walls and a roof to a homeowner. The seller, unless he or she is unusually objective, can't avoid feeling that the home has a special intrinsic value due to its personal history.

Your job is to bring clarity, logic and truth to the transaction. By having an informal appraisal done on the home, by scouting the location thoroughly, by having the home inspected, by researching all there is to know about this home and its neighborhood, you'll have reams of hard factual data that will carry more weight in the negotiation than all the emotional baggage the seller brings to it.

Even so, you'll treat the home with the proper degree of respect. Remember that this is, to the seller, more than a house. You're not going to pay for this emotional attachment in dollar and cents, but you should nevertheless be prepared to acknowledge it to the buyer. So much of the home-buying process is wrapped up in the egos of buyer and seller. A seller can't help but feel that an attack on his price is an assault on him or herself. You must be ready to validate the seller's feelings for the home through your words and actions, but not through increases in your offer. Bear in mind the fact that the seller is feeling more stress than you are.

In such a situation, it's crucial that you sublimate your own emotions. Remember, there are thousands of homes on the market, and hundreds more coming on the market each day. If a home is priced out of your league, and if, after investigation you find that its fair market value is still beyond your reach, then that home just isn't for you. Throughout the negotiating process, you possess the awesome power of being able to walk away. And don't try to lowball your way to a steal of the home. It won't work. Sellers and brokers will know what you're up to, and may be able to take advantage of you. Your aim at all times is to be fair.

That doesn't mean that you will pay the asking price. Fairness is a two-way street. Meeting the asking price isn't fair to the buyer, since it forces no movement on the seller's part. In order that there be true fairness in the negotiating process, there must be movement on both sides.

A seller places a home on the market at a price that has built into it both a profit for the seller and a 6 percent commission for the broker. Sellers are buffeted by brokers who often puff up the value of the home in order to get the listing. All the information that a seller gets is distorted by his own dreams and his broker's guile. Your responsibility in a fair negotiation is to bring the seller back down to earth—gently—by drawing his or her attention to the facts and data that are the foundation of the market value of the home. In the real estate negotiation, knowledge truly is power.

PREPARING FOR THE NEGOTIATION

To repeat: The most important part of the negotiation takes place before you actually make the first offer. To gauge accurately how much to offer for a home, you must learn all you can about the seller as well as the home.

By studying the location in depth (Chapter Six) and analyzing the site itself (Chapter Seven), you have become an expert on this particular home. Once you have decided that this particular home meets your priorities needs and wants, and that it falls into your affordability range, you'll still have to do some further investigation.

The key to determining the fair market value of a home is to find out what comparable homes have sold for in the past few weeks or months. Either by consulting with a knowledgeable (and obviously disinterested) broker, or by touring the offerings in the neighborhood, you may be able to find accurate comparables. But to have a truly firm knowledge of market value through the comparables, you will have to consult with an expert in comparables—an appraiser.

We have seen (in Chapter Seven) how to find an appraiser who has expertise in your potential home's area. Make an appointment with this appraiser and advise him or her that you will be looking for an expert opinion on the value of a home in the area. Give the appraiser the exact location of the home in question, as well as the details on the size of the home, the number of bedrooms and bathrooms, and any other details that affect value.

The appraiser will in all likelihood consult records and find the three most recent comparable sales in the building or neighborhood. He or she may visit the home in question and determine whether it is worth more or less than the average selling price of the three comparable sales. If it has only two bedrooms and one bathroom, and the other recent sales had three bedrooms and two baths, the appraiser will quote a lower price. If it has four bedrooms and two and one-half baths, the appraiser will quote a higher price.

This appraisal is similar to the bank's appraisal for a mortgage, but is more studied, since it is undertaken for a different reason. The bank is only concerned that you are not paying too much. If the home isn't worth as much as you pay for it, and then you default on your mortgage, the bank might have to sell the home for a loss. Their appraisal is a fail-safe maneuver, not a thoroughgoing fact-finding endeavor. Your appraisal is a tool to pin down the actual value of the home in order to make a sensible offer.

With this final piece of intelligence about the home itself safely tucked away in your pocket, you now have to begin finding out about the seller. The first place to find this information is the broker.

Try to find out from the seller or broker why the home is up for sale. Is the seller moving to a larger home—buying up, since his or her family or income is growing? Or moving to a smaller home—buying down, since the family or income has shrunk? Discover all you can about the seller's motivations. Is he moving to a new job in another city? Is he retiring? If the seller has a time deadline looming over his head, you can use that information to your advantage—perhaps by offering a speedy closing in exchange for a price concession. You can obtain this information simply by asking the broker these questions, or by tactfully questioning the seller about his or her future plans.

Discover what type of person the seller is. Is he stubborn? does he have experience in negotiating, perhaps through business? Is he an amateur painter, a gourmet cook, a collector of pottery? All this can be gleaned either from the broker, or through conversations with the neighbors, or by a studied tour of the home. Look at the accessories around the house. Check the titles of books on the shelves, and magazines on coffee tables. Is there an extensive wine rack? Are the ashtrays overflowing with cigarette butts? Do you see piles of unpaid bills on the kitchen table? What kind of of artwork is on the walls? Any information you can gather about "the other side" in the transaction can help you set your strategy. By knowing the person on the other side of the table, you can attempt to address his or her needs. Also, the more you know about the other side, the more comfortable and confident you will feel when it comes time to negotiate.

Of course this advice applies only if you are dealing with the seller in person. That is usually desirable, but sometimes impossible. If the seller is out of town, you may have to deal with a relative or an attorney. Sometimes, even though the seller is available, he or she may be so scared to negotiate that he or she will delegate all authority to the lawyer. I've conducted negotiations with sellers—even reaching what appeared to be agreements—only to discover that the person or persons I was bargaining with had no power to make a decision. Always try to prequalify the negotiator to make sure that he is in the position to make the final decisions.

FORMULATING AND CONVEYING THE OFFER

Never meet the price asked by the seller, even if your analysis shows that it is below the appraiser's value judgment. If a home has just come onto the market and you meet the asking price, the seller will, more often than not, pull the home off the market and boost his asking price. This will be done on the assumption that the initial price was too low. In addition, by meeting the asking price, you preclude a fair negotiation. The seller has set the asking price at a level higher than he or she is willing to accept. By meeting it, you are not forcing the seller to move at all. Remember: Fair negotiation requires both sides to move to a middle ground.

In formulating your offer, you should refer back to your conversation with the appraiser about comparables and the fair market value of the home in question. Appraisers often assign a 10 percent value range—from $90,000 to $110,000, for example—rather than say that the home is worth $100,000.

It's safe to assume that the seller has set his asking price above the range cited by the appraiser. Our counteroffer should be 10 percent below the low end of the appraised range. This gives both sides an opportunity to move toward fair market value, letting vagaries of the negotiation determine the selling price.

If the seller's asking price is inside the market value range, you should still respond with a counter offer 10 percent below the range. In this way you're setting the stage for the selling price to come out near the low end.

Sellers aren't always as aware of market value as buyers are. If you find that the asking price is below the market range, don't get overanxious and meet it. Respond with a counteroffer 10 percent below the asking price, in order to push the figure down even more.

By having your lawyer do an informal title search on the property while you are negotiating, you may be able to use the seller's greed against him. If, for example, you find that the seller is trying to make a profit in excess of 100% over 2 years, as I once discovered, you can work up some righteous indignation and perhaps shame him into a concession.

In the midst of the negotiation it's essential to remember the affordability figure you came up with earlier. While it's possible to bargain the seller of your dream home to a price you can afford, it's also possible to get caught up in the emotion of the purchase. I'd advise you not to enter into the negotiations for the purchase of any home that has a market range more than 20 percent above your affordability figure.

Always keep your bottom-line figure firmly in hand. Never enter into any negotiation without a "drop dead price."

Stick to it. Perhaps you should write it down somewhere, and glance at it occasionally. You have stretched and cut back and sacrificed in coming up with the maximum you can afford. Now—embroiled as you are in the heat of negotiation—is not the time to stretch any further. If a broker says that this is the only home for you he is lying. It is probably the only home *he* has for you. There are lots of other homes out there, and lots of other brokers.

Price negotiations tend to move toward a compromise middle ground, somewhere between the first offer and the counteroffer. Because of this, your initial offer sets the stage for the rest of the process. Often experts can foresee the end result of a negotiation long before it is reached. They will be able to predict the sale price as long as both sides remain consistent in their negotiating posture.

Make sure that you can supply a reason for your offer. If you have found some defects in the home, perhaps you should point them out—but gently. Never characterize the seller's price in any way. Instead, back up your offer with facts. Tell the seller or the broker about your informal appraisal, leaving out the word "informal." Inform them of the comparables you've learned about. Indicate that your offer is a bit lower since the home in question, say, has two bedrooms instead of the three in one of the comparables. Mention that while the home is "beautiful," you may still have to have a new paint job, or remodel the bathrooms and kitchen. Place the onus on your own wants and needs; don't characterize the price as too high, or the home as too small.

By the way, if the broker or seller starts touting potential alterations in the house, realize that they are just that, potentials. Also, if they point out that a fireplace would look great in the living room, don't add a dime extra for that possibility when you are formulating your offer. You are buying the home as it exists now, not as it will look five years and $50,000 later.

Once you have reached a decision on your offer, based on facts and hard data, you have to find a way to convey it to the seller.

If the seller is represented by a real estate broker, you will be forced to convey the offer through the broker. That isn't necessarily a bad route. Sometimes the broker is the best conduit for a negotiation. This is particularly true if he or she is a true professional, serving the deal and not just the seller. A broker may even serve as a double agent, gathering information for you, reporting on the seller's feelings and strategies. In addition, the broker can serve as a screen between the two parties, giving each some room for face saving. A good broker will take the blame for objectionable parts of the negotiation. Also, brokers are bound by a code of ethics. They must communicate all offers to the seller. If the broker says the offer is too low, insist that it be conveyed anyway, and that it be accompanied by your reasons. If you discover that the broker has lied to you, go around him. Don't give him a second chance to lie to you. Don't let a deal fall apart because the broker is incompetent. Insist on seeing the seller yourself.

If there is no broker in the deal, or if you have had to bypass an incompetent one, present your offer directly to the seller. At that time, be prepared to negotiate on the spot and signal that willingness. Present the offer in person at the home. Make yourself physically comfortable. Take your time. Ask for a glass of water. Spread out some notes and papers. Ask to hang up your coat or jacket. Signal, in as many ways as possible, that you are ready to make a deal.

Don't act stern and hard. Maintain a good humor. Smiling and appearing friendly will go far toward cutting down the undercurrent of aggression that invariably surrounds a deal. You want to make clear that you can be trusted. Show your concern for the needs of the other side. Listen intently. Smile. Open your hands and your arms. Ask for help in reaching an agreement. Make clear that you and the seller are partners in reaching an agreement. The entire real estate transaction is so often shrouded in fear and distrust. Remember, most of us approach negotiation as if it were a sinister art, enacted to bamboozle and swindle—the very antithesis of fairness and honesty. By taking charge of the situation and putting the seller at ease, you can go a long way toward eliminating his fear and distrust. Don't approach the real estate negotiation—or any negotiation, for that matter—from a self-centered point of view. Knowledge of and respect for our opponents' needs, wants and feelings, are the secret weapons of a skilled negotiator.

Regardless of who is doing the negotiating, remember that it is you who are pulling the strings. By all means accept advice from attorneys, accountants, appraisers, even brokers—but remember that you are the one who will be signing the mortgage checks. No one can tell you what to pay. In fair negotiating, it is your responsibility to look out for yourself.

If you find that you are competing with another potential buyer, get out of the process. You want to be the only game in town. Ask that you be contacted once the negotiations with another buyer are completed. Refuse to take part in a contest. This is a fair negotiation. You aren't looking to win and neither should the seller. Stress that you are serious about the house, and then let the seller's urgency work on your behalf.

INCREMENTAL NEGOTIATIONS

The next step in the negotiation is the counteroffer—the seller's response to your initial offer. To start off with, don't get upset if there no response. Indicate, to either the broker or the seller, that you are willing to negotiate and await a response. An astute seller will always respond, even if only to say that he is willing to deal with "serious bids." If your offer was based on hard data, now is the time to provide it to an unresponsive seller. If there are significant problems with the property, necessitating expenses on your part, provide a list to the seller, totalling up the necessary repairs, and include a copy of the appraisal with references to comparable sales.

Still no response? Then you are probably dealing with a seller who has only been testing the waters, or who isn't really serious about selling for a fair price. Many sellers put homes on the market at their "dream price," and if they are unable to get it, refuse to budge. Ask them if you are to interpret this refusal to move as a sign that they aren't interested in negotiating. If this elicits no response, walk away from the deal. You'll probably hear from the broker again. Advise the seller or broker that when the process is open to negotiation, you may still be interested. But tell him or her that until then, you will be looking for another, more amenable seller.

Once you have received a response to your offer, study it

carefully. Brokers call the counteroffer "the great unzipping." In general, sellers come back with a number that indicates they will accept the midpoint between the first offer and the counteroffer. Ask for some rationale for their new price, in light of the documentation and comparables that you have studied. Is their home larger? In better condition? Make sure that they give you a reason for their new price. Remind them that you are willing to pay market value, but are curious as to how they have arrived at their number.

Respond to the counteroffer with another incremental increase in your offer, aiming to pin down that middle ground. Offer either more factual data or a good reason for your offer once again. At every step in the process, you will be basing your offers on hard and factual data, which will transform the negotiation from emotional haggling to rational discussion and compromise.

If you find that the seller makes frequent, small concessions in price, respond in kind. When the seller makes many concessions, this indicates that he is desperate to sell, or uncomfortable with his price. If a seller makes significant concessions, respond with significant concessions of your own. This could indicate that the seller is anxious to close a fair deal quickly. Take advantage of this by also moving steadily and quickly.

Never bid against yourself. If you fail to get a response, ask if the last counteroffer was the seller's final price concession. Generally, you will be able to sense when the negotiation is entering the final stages by noting how the concessions on both sides are becoming smaller and smaller. But never follow up your own offer with another.

But even this rule may have to be broken on occasion.

When I was negotiating my daughter's purchase of a lovely Vermont farm, I followed all the rules. My increments were based on the seller's increments and as the negotiation went on I could see that we were going to settle midway on a price between our numbers. Suddenly, the seller stopped dead in his tracks. I couldn't understand it. All the signs had pointed to a successful negotiation. Yet my latest offer stood unanswered. The broker, who was acting as intermediary, told me that the seller was standing on his last price.

Without bidding against myself I had to come up with some way of reactivating the deal. I decided to break the deadlock by stating the obvious. I told the broker to relay to the seller that I was willing to raise my price if he was willing to lower his. In other words, I'm willing to negotiate if you are. This simple technique saved the day. And I'm amazed at how many times it has worked for me since.

Never signal your own bottom line to the seller of the broker. First, they won't believe you. Second, they will start pushing you to offer your top price as soon as they are aware of it. Keep your drop dead price a secret from the other side, but be sure to keep it foremost in your own mind. Make smaller concessions the closer you get to it. And never, *never* go beyond it. To reiterate a key point: all your stretching should be done in advance, during the affordability stage, not during negotiation.

You must always be prepared to walk away from the deal, otherwise you will fail as a negotiator. There is no one home you can't live without. In fact, in your chosen location there are probably a handful that would be fine purchases. Let me repeat: Don't fall in love with a home until you own it. Any seller who senses that you have already fallen in love with his home and don't want to lose it will rake you over the coals. It's just like asking for a raise. If your boss suspects you have another job lined up, he'll be more likely to give you the raise.

If both sides keep their eyes trained on the ball, and deal with the price as an abstract number rather than an emotional issue, you should be able to reach an agreement. But if you do find yourself at an impasse, don't give up. Instead, get creative.

CREATIVE NEGOTIATING TO AVOID AN IMPASSE

Schedule a sit-down meeting with the seller. Present your case and your data once more. Express your sincere interest in the house, as well as your desire to reach a fair agreement.

There is a tendency to reach a deal once both parties have taken the time and made the effort to sit down together. Both the seller and the broker will have invested a great deal of energy in the process. They won't want to see it wasted.

If there is an impasse in the negotiation, the broker can sometimes be persuaded to cut back on his fee. Say to the broker that you need his help. Ask if he cares about the deal. (Of course he does—he gets his money only if the deal goes through.) Suggest that all of the parties work together and make sacrifices in the interest of reaching an agreement. The longer the negotiation has gone on, the more likely the broker will be to cut a deal.

Another way of breaking an impasse on price is to introduce new elements in the deal. This is achieved by turning it into a "mosaic," rather than just a dollar issue.

Creative financing can be a big help in jumping an obstacle. Ask the seller to finance the deal in exchange for accepting his most recent offer. He can "take back" a mortgage at a rate of interest that is 1 or 2 percent less than the rate a bank would offer. Over the life of the mortgage, you may actually save the difference in price which you made up. Perhaps you can convince the seller that a lifelong annuity would fit his or her needs better than a lump sum payment. Together you can tailor a mortgage to the seller's financial needs, reducing the tax that he'll have to pay on the sale.

Another option open to you is to have the seller finance only the difference between your best offer and his best price—say $5,000. You can agree to accept his price, but stipulate that the added dollars not come due for five years, and that no interest be charged. This option allows the seller to save face by claiming that he has gotten his price, while giving you enough time either to save or borrow the added amount. A side benefit is that the $5,000 debt actually drops in cost over the five years, thanks to inflation and to the fact that during that time the money could be earning interest for you.

Alternatively, you could offer to sign a lease with an option to buy at his price after a set period of time. In that way, you are getting possession without buying, and still preventing anyone else from buying. By the time you have to exercise the option, your affordability will have gone up, as will the value of the house.

There are permutations upon permutations for creative financing. (I'll discuss other forms with you in Chapter Thirteen, when I speak of the mortgage process.) Here's where your accountant and attorney can be of great help. Be sure to bypass the broker when you are negotiating any of these creative options. Brokers only receive their fee upon the sale of the home. Brokers won't be pleased that they'll have to wait five years for payment, even if everyone else is ecstatic about the creative deal.

Instead of creative financing, you can ask for added value. A developer, for example, may be more apt to add a fireplace or make a basement bigger, rather than concede on price. Suggest that you will pay the price the seller wants on the condition that the kitchen is remodeled, the bathroom updated, or the entire home is painted.

As an incentive for the seller to make the final concession, you could offer a speedy closing. If you already have a mortgage in your pocket, tell the broker or seller. Advise him that you can go to contract in forty-eight hours. Speed is worth money to the seller, since every day your money isn't in his or her bank account, interest income is lost.

None of these techniques violates our original strategy. We are simply compensating for the fact that the seller has increased the price above either the fair market value or our ability to pay. We're trying to formulate a deal in which the amount they will accept is brought into line with what we can afford to pay and what the home is actually worth. It's all part of the fair negotiating process.

Negotiating the purchase of a home requires a firm foundation in facts about the home in question; an understanding of the seller's needs, wants and motivations; and a flexible, open-minded approach toward combining dollars with other items of value.

Yet even the fairest and most creative negotiating techniques won't guarantee that you will be able to reach an agreement on price with a seller. There are times when a combination of voluminous data, creative financing and savvy negotiating will fail to sway stubborn sellers. If the deal falls through, don't mourn. I have found that the deals that fail were usually meant to fail. In the long run, you'll be better off. When a deal falls through, don't regard it as a rejection. Heave a deep sigh, draw in your forces, collect your thoughts, review why things went wrong, learn from any mistakes you may have made and start over. Go back to Chapter Eight and begin on another hunt.

CHAPTER TEN

THE
INSPECTION
REPORT

When you have eliminated the
impossible,
whatever remains, however
improbable,
must be the truth.
SIR ARTHUR CONAN DOYLE

While your first and second tours will help uncover problems and possible money traps in the home, it is absolutely essential that a professional engineer or house inspector examine the premises and prepare a report for you. Sellers will spare no effort in camouflaging flaws in the home, and brokers, anxious for a sale, won't be forthcoming with any information they may have about the leaky roof, damp basement, or the eroding mountain slope.

An inspecting engineer can examine all of the components that make up the envelope and operating systems of the house. While your newly sharpened eye may be able to spot obvious flaws in the roof, exterior walls or foundation of the home, only a trained inspecting engineer can tell for sure if that slight sag in the roof is a planned drainage feature, a sign of deferred maintenance or an omen of imminent collapse. An engineer is trained to recognize inadequate plumbing, electrical and heating systems. And having examined the entire home, a good inspecting engineer will be able to determine which repairs will have to be made in the near future, and estimate what those repairs will cost.

Don't accept the seller's or broker's claims that an inspection isn't necessary, or that one has been done in the near past. Every previously occupied home should be inspected by potential purchasers, and the inspection should be carried out by a professional hired by the buyer, not the seller or broker. And don't hire anyone recommended by the seller or broker. You don't want your inspecting engineer beholden to the owner or broker in any way. Without casting aspersions on the integrity of inspectors, it is only human nature not to bite the hand that feeds you. An inspector who depends on broker referrals for his bread and butter will not be known for his eagle eye and critical nature. Yet despite this obvious conflict of interest, the average buyer hires an inspector based on the broker's recommendation.

As we noted in Chapter Seven, an inspecting engineer should be selected based on an attorney's recommendations. You are looking for the most experienced engineer you can find—someone who knows both the business in general, and your location in particular. While homes are quite similar all over the country, the problems and traps an inspecting engineer looks for vary from geographic region to region. For example, in the Pacific Northwest inspectors are always on the outlook for dampness and flooding due to the heavy rainfall. In the Southwest dryness and heat are the scourges of homes. In Southern California, engineers have to check for earthquake damage, and judge how much fault or fracture stress a home could sustain. In the north central part of the country, engineers will be looking for adequate insulation from the severe cold, both in the living spaces and in the plumbing and heating spaces. In the Southeast the problem is high temperatures.

Look for someone who works full-time, not nights. It may be necessary to use a part-timer for an apartment inspection, since few firms offer the service, but make sure the inspection is done during the day on the weekend.

You want an engineer who has experience inspecting your specific type of home. If you are moving into an apartment, you'll want your inspector to have gone through the boiler rooms of many an apartment building. You don't want to be a suburban inspector's first job in the central city. Likewise, an engineer trained and experienced in high-rise apartment building construction won't be at the top of his game inspecting a single-family suburban home. Look for a specialist.

Make sure the inspector is licensed by the state, either as an engineer or architect. This won't guarantee that his or her work will be equal to your demands, but it will at least assure you of some recourse should the relationship foul up. Licensed professionals are accountable to the state and have a stake in playing the game ethically.

Ask for samples of past inspections. While they will have little bearing on the specifics of your home, other inspection reports will show you how deeply the inspector probes, how exacting his standards are, and how specific his or her comments are.

Make sure that the inspection report is, first, in writing. Without a written report, negotiations based on inspection data will be very difficult. Next, make sure that the inspector does more than just check off good, fair or poor on a standardized list of features. While all inspectors use checklists to ensure that they don't overlook anything, a top pro will preface the checklist with an abstract, briefly summarizing the home's condition, and then a longer narrative, going over, item by item, the condition of the home's envelope and systems.

Look to see if the inspecting engineer has listed the estimated costs for replacing or repairing defects in the home. Some inspectors make it a standard part of their package. Others hesitate to make projections. You will want such estimates, and in fact, should be willing to pay a slightly higher fee, if asked, for these numbers.

Ask the inspecting engineer if you can accompany him on the inspection tour. Most inspectors will encourage your participation, since it allows them more opportunities to expand on their comments. Any inspector who doesn't like company isn't working very hard at his job. While accompanying the inspector on his rounds, don't interfere, but feel free to ask any questions that occur to you.

References, or the names of the last three clients of an inspector, should be acquired and checked into. Ask your attorney and accountant if they have heard anything about this engineer. Reputations are important. Other pros' opinions can be good hints as to your engineer's standing in his profession.

The inspection itself will take between one and two hours and will cost anywhere from $125 to $300, not including travel, laboratory work or soil borings if necessary.

The only time when an inspecting engineer may not be necessary is at the purchase of a brand new home. An inspector may be able to tell you about the quality of workmanship and materials, but there is no sign of wear or weathering by which to judge the degree of maintenance or the durability of the structure. When buying new homes, it is better to spend your money and time on investigating the builder of the home, checking into his past projects, reputation, reliability and responsibility.

An inspector should be in place on your team as soon as you begin the hunt for a home. He or she should be prepared to leap into action within forty-eight hours of your call. You aren't going to wait until a contract has been signed to have the home inspected. Your engineer will be on the job during the negotiation, right after your offer has been accepted.

It has become traditional in many parts of the country to go directly to contract on a home without first having an inspection. Attorneys write into the contract a clause making the agreement subject to a positive inspection report. You, however, will want an inspection made before the contract is ironed out. If the inspection turns up anything that needs repair work and an investment of dollars, you want to be able to introduce that fact into the contract negotiation before the purchase price is set in.

READING THE INSPECTION REPORT

The most important thing to remember when reading an inspection report, or when discussing the results with the engineer, is that there is no such thing as a passing or failing grade. It is not the job of the engineer to tell you whether or not to buy the home. All he or she can do is point out defects or areas where maintenance has been deferred, and then estimate how much it will cost to repair or bring up to code. Many inspectors recount tales of the prospective owners following them around the home, pleading, almost begging the inspector to overlook some problems. Remember one of our cardinal rules of home buying: Don't fall in love with a home until you own it. An inspection should be an unbiased examination of the home—uninfluenced by broker, seller or buyer.

Most inspection reports will begin with a brief description of how the inspection was performed and what was and was not included. Most engineers will not mention obvious cracks in concrete or woodwork that needs repainting unless they are indicative of more complex problems that aren't readily apparent to home buyers. In addition, engineers will not examine each appliance, instead leaving it up the home buyer to check their condition. Inspections concentrate on the condition of the envelope of the home (roof, walls, windows, foundation) and the operating systems of the home (heating, electrical and plumbing). Generally, the report will indicate that the inspection was a visual one, performed under the standards and guidelines of either the American Society of Home Inspectors or some other national organization.

Many reports will include a disclaimer noting that the findings are based on observable, unconcealed structural conditions, adding that the inspector could not tear up carpet, puncture walls or move furniture. Inspections do not guarantee or warrant the condition of the home, and most reports will include wording to that effect. In addition, inspection reports will not be looking for building code violations, and the disclaimer will note that a further, code-based inspection may be necessary. Reports also note that they do not preclude the presence of possible problems with toxic materials or gases in inaccessible areas, or the presence of chemicals or gases, for which inspections are not normally carried out. Inspectors, looking to ensure that they suffer no liability from possible problems, will insist on making separate inspections for possible toxic problems, such as radon or asbestos. If there is a pool that requires inspection, you may need to speak to a specialist. The only additional inspection that most engineers will make is a simple termite search conducted during the home inspection or subsequently.

After the disclaimers, the report will then give a narrative discussion of the condition of the home, broken down into separate sections dealing with the foundation, general structure, presence or absence of termites, crawl space or basement, roof condition, general exterior condition, windows, garage, condition of interior surfaces and systems, heating system, hot water, electrical, plumbing, attic and insulation.

Carefully read each section of the report, noting any recommendations that are made by the inspector. Have a pen in hand and underline any mention of repairs that need to be made. For example, an analysis of the heating system might mention that the boiler and water heater are undersized for the home. Note the age of the pipes and what they are made of. A good engineer will then analyze how much longer they can be expected to remain serviceable and how much they will cost to replace. Water stains should be noted and causes may be speculated on. Comments on the layout and zone structure of the heating plant will help determine which rooms will be cold in winter. Suggested improvements should be listed, along with the cost of each. Possible environmental hazards, such as asbestos, may be noted, but don't expect the engineer to go out on a limb without specific instructions to search for them.

Throughout the report, the engineer will touch on areas that may require substantial investment in the future. If insulation is inadequate, an engineer will note that a major expense may be looming on the horizon. Suggestions for more efficient maintenance and home operation may be offered in the report, such as the installation of glass fireplace doors to cut down on heat loss, or the replacement of old damaged double-hung windows with new thermopane models.

Termite information will be found both in the body of the report, and on a separate sheet called a termite certificate. This government form is the standard reporting device for home inspectors doing an insect search. Any inaccessibility will be noted. An evaluation based on visual evidence will be provided. The form allows inspectors to choose between visible evidence of damage with no measures taken, no visible evidence, visible evidence with measures taken, visible damage observed, and visible evidence of previously active, now eliminated insect problems.

Most inspecting engineers will sum up their observations in a brief abstract that notes that the home is generally in poor, fair, good, or exceptional condition. This judgment will not be a recommendation to buy or an encouragement to abandon the deal. Instead, inspectors look to provide buyers with information on which to make their own informed decision. When pressed, inspecting engineers may note that they don't consider the property a good buy, but most engineers will shy away from any advice on buying, leaving that up to you.

Inspection reports on multifamily dwellings, such as co-op and condo apartments, will include information on any work that will have to be done to the common areas of the building, such as exterior, lobby, elevator, as well as the specific apartment. Multifamily home inspections will focus on areas that could cause the maintenance or common charges to the potential owner to jump significantly. A good engineer can determine what work will have to be done to the building in the next five years, and estimate what effect that will have on the monthly charges a potential owner will be paying. Repairs necessary in the particular unit will also be discussed. But since the majority of maintenance work needed in any home is in the operating systems or envelope—in a multi-family dwelling, the common areas—they will be the most prominent part of the engineer's search.

Every inspection report should include the checklist used during the actual search of the home. Look for additional comments on the checklist. Simply circling one of the choices under each category may ensure that all the bases are covered, but it doesn't indicate that thought went into either the original inspection, or the writing of the report. Check for additional information in the areas left for remarks and comments. Examine the description of the siting of the home on the lot. Look for the orientation. The parts of the checklist dealing with interior rooms should be broken down to very specific categories, such as electrical outlets and fixtures.

Throughout the inspection report, look for hints of unspoken worries or problems. Remember, engineers won't be advising on the purchase of the home. They will, however, through their choice of words, tip you off to their own feelings on the matter. Look for words like "fine," "safe," and "secure" in the narrative account. Words such as marginal, temporary, and shoddy should set off red lights in your head, no matter how cheap you think you're getting the property.

The inspection report isn't the final word in making a buying decision. It won't tell you if you are buying a wonderful home or a fabulous investment. It is, however, the most unbiased and foolproof means to avoid buying a lemon. By looking out for future problems, engineers can make sure that you aren't taken advantage of or railroaded by unscrupulous sellers or brokers. It's your safety net, not an insurance policy. Make sure you check it for holes. It's a long drop from the joy of moving into a wonderful home to the hiring of a plumber to replace the entire water system.

CHAPTER ELEVEN

THE
CONTRACT

Festina lente.
(Make haste slowly)
SUETONIUS

One of the great misconceptions about the home-buying transaction is that the title closing is legally the important part of the deal. Actually, the closing (as I will show in Chapter Thirteen) is little more than a prearranged ritualistic exchange of dollars and deeds. The contract is actually the heart of the deal, intellectually as well as legally. But interestingly enough, the contract is also the most underemphasized part of the deal. All across America, brokers and escrow agents are preaching that attorneys only mess up deals, pollute the otherwise clear water of the transaction and add to costs and delays. The brokers' real estate lobby has even succeeded in getting some state legislatures to rewrite home-buying regulations to make attorneys superfluous. They are succeeding in turning the real estate contract into a mere formality. Nothing could be worse for the home buyer.

I have had clients swagger into my office proudly waving what they thought was a *binder* that reserved a "great deal" and that took the home off the market so they could have time to mull over the feasibility of a purchase. They confidently ordered me to proceed now with the rest of the transaction and "take care of the details." All I can do is shake my head and inform them that their wonderful "reservation" document is actually a *binding contract* to buy the home, containing all the necessary aspects of a legally enforceable agreement, without any of the provisions that normally protect a buyer. There's almost nothing I can do to help them except plead that they lacked contractual capacity (i.e., were insane) when they signed the document. I then offer them a box of Kleenex.

Afraid of being depicted as deal busters, attorneys in the United States have sat back and abdicated their role in the drafting and scrutiny of the real estate contract. That is the bad news for the buyers. Why would the lawyers let this happen? In part, because of laziness. Good, customized real estate contracts—the type we want—are complicated documents, requiring that the attorney do more than simply balance the seller-biased forms with a mollifying rider. In fact, they should be going further, as you will realize once you have read this chapter. Secondly, attorneys can now sit back and wait for these broker-orchestrated contracts to fall apart and then ride to the rescue. The faculty contracts end up in court, and the lawyers collect a bigger fee than they would have if they had been involved in the initial drafting of the agreement.

The contract is the heart, the very cornerstone, of the transaction. If a contract falls through, everything that you have done before, each and every step you have taken on the road to home ownership, will be for naught. The contract should thoroughly stipulate all the rights and responsibilities of both buyer and seller, while effectively freezing the home on the market. It thus ensures that until your attempt to buy has either succeeded or fallen through, no one else can buy the home, no matter how high a new offer they make.

As with much of our real estate law, the written contract for the exchange of property originated in English Common Law. Judges had great difficulty deciding cases in which two individuals disagreed about the basic facts of an agreement. In order to provide a basis for decisions, the courts established the Statute of Frauds, which stipulated that certain agreements—including the exchange of real estate—in order to be enforceable, must be in writing.

But nowhere in the historic English Statute of Frauds or in any of the statutes of any state in the U.S., does it say how that contract should be written. Many brokers, sellers and even some not-so-savvy lawyers, will tell you that there is a standard form for the real estate contract, in which you and the seller can simply fill in the blanks. In some states, brokers will even hand prospective buyers forms for making an offer which, upon acceptance by the seller, become binding contracts.

Stay away from any contract that is not customized to fit your particular needs and wants. The standard forms are written by companies that write forms, not by attorneys. And they never—I repeat, never—treat the buyer fairly. Often the forms are deliberately slanted toward the seller, in so far as they streamline by including as few conditions as possible. Almost all are written by or for organizations that are concerned only with closing deals.

Competent attorneys have standard riders, written either by themselves or copied from someone else, which help balance the transaction. But that isn't sufficient for our purposes. Remember out motto: Your deal is a customized one. Every home, every seller and every buyer is unique. So should every contract be unique.

An adequate contract is essential to "winning" in the home-buying war. The contract takes the property off the market and defines clearly the responsibilities of both parties. You have first claim on the property, regardless of any subsequent offers or bids that the seller may receive.

Beyond that, the contract spells out a series of rights and responsibilities for both buyer and seller. It gives the seller the responsibility to do the following: maintain the home during the period of time between contract and title in its existing condition; make good on any problems that your inspection has uncovered that they had previously agreed to remedy or repair; deliver clear title (free of the claims of others) on the date specified; maintain the appliances and major systems, such as heating and plumbing; allow for an inspection prior to closing; pay all taxes and expenses until closing; and pay the broker's commission, if any.

Getting a clear title isn't always easy. Claims against the seller for back taxes by the IRS, the state or the local government can complicate and encumber the title. In addition, a title search will ensure that in the chain of title (the ongoing series of deeds from the original owner of the property to the current owner), no third party has been given a special property right. In 1790, it's quite possible that an adjacent property owner was granted the right to water horses at your stream or graze in your pasture. Today, however, that special right may have evolved into a legitimate claim by a neighbor that he owns a right of way through your back yard.

The contract will specify what type of deed the seller will be passing on to you. A "quit claim" deed is the minimum possible, and it is not the one for you. Under a quit claim deed the seller bears no responsibility for any title problems that develop, but conveys no more or less than what he or she has. A more protective type of deed is the "bargain and sale with covenants against grantors acts," in which the seller guarantees he did nothing to create claims against the property by others, but offers no responsibility for his predecessors. (That will be up to your title company.) Most potent is the "full covenant and warranty" deed, in which the seller takes responsibility for the entire chain of title. It isn't really necessary for us to go after that one since the title company will be in effect taking responsibility for all past owners.

Along with these responsibilities, the seller also acquires certain rights under the contract: to receive the price agreed to at the time agreed to; and to be reimbursed for any prepaid expenses. These might include property taxes for the period after you've taken possession, and for any fuel oil that was in the tank when you moved in.

The writing of the contract actually opens up another opportunity to negotiate. Once the process of working out the contract has begun, the seller and his attorney will almost certainly fixate on you and your concerns, since by now his greatest fear is that you pull out. As soon as you reached an agreement on price, the seller in all likelihood had already started counting the dollars and arranging for his new shelter. In fact, time may be of the essence to the seller, who may very well have a deadline to close on his own new purchase. He is itching to get the contract signed and move on the closing. You can use this pressure to your advantage and ask for some incidental points which you may have either forgotten about, or lost out on, during the original negotiation.

While the procedure varies somewhat from state to state, it is generally the seller's attorney who draws up the contract. Don't worry. At this point it's actually better to be on the receiving end. You and your attorney are in the enviable position of being able to sit back and take potshots at the seller's proposed contract. You might strike out objectionable clauses, for example, and insert those of your own. It's much harder to defend a proposed contract than it is to assault one.

Sellers and their attorneys will put pressure on you to sit down with them and draw up and sign a contract in one afternoon. Refuse graciously. Beg off, citing other commitments. Do anything to get out of an instant contract. For once, the U.S. Postal Service is your ally. With each delay, the hook sinks a little bit deeper into the seller, giving you a bit more power.

It is common practice for the seller's attorney to send the proposed contract to your attorney. Make sure that you get a copy as well. Make an appointment and go directly to your attorney's office. You are going to make sure that you understand every clause, notation or set of initials in the agreement. And you'll also make sure that it addresses certain concerns.

Before we get into the minutiae and extra clauses to look for, let's examine the standard parts of the contract.

In order to be a legally binding real estate contract, the instrument must be dated. The full names of the buyer and of every seller must be spelled out in full. Mr. and Mrs. Joe Buyer isn't good enough. Have it read Mr. and Mrs. Joe and Jane Buyer. And to make doubly sure, the addresses of all the parties should also be included.

The exact location should be described as accurately as possible in the contract. The seller's deed should have a legal definition of the location, defining the configuration of the property by *metes* (the physical measurements in feet) and *bounds* (the compass direction of the boundary lines.) Your contract's definition of the property's location should also include the house number and street address used by the post office. If no address is available, make sure that the lot and block number appearing on the municipal planning map are included. If you are purchasing a co-op or condo apartment, make sure that the apartment number is included in the location description. When buying a co-op, you also want the number of shares purchased to be indicated prominently.

A provision in the contract should cover the legal status of the home. Insist that sellers turn over a certificate of occupancy at the closing, and also make sure that your attorney sees a copy of it well before the closing day. A certificate of occupancy will ensure that the home was built according to the municipal building code. It will also show if the home is legally a single-family, two-family or multifamily residence.

A date and time for the closing of title must be written into the contract. While this can be changed later—and probably will be—it is mandatory. In legal contracts there are three ways to which date and time deadlines are referred: "on," "on or about," and "time is of the essence." Sellers want the latter. If you sign a contract that specifies a closing date with the phrase "time is of the essence," you can be found in default if you don't close exactly on that day, for any reason up to and including illness, death and Armageddon. Instruct your attorney to change any references to "time is of the essence" to "on or about." This will legally give you a reasonable amount of time to perform an action. Sellers won't like it, but you'll be protected. For the same reason, make it a rule to change every mention of the number of days you have to take an action to the same number of **business** days.

The purchase price, and exactly how it will be paid, must be indicated in the contract. If the buyer is paying $100,000 for a home, and $10,000 will be delivered in cash as a deposit at the signing of the contract (with the rest coming from a mortgage at the title closing), that must be spelled out in writing. If the seller is taking back a mortgage, that also must be written into the contractual description of the purchase price. Furthermore, the contract should state what types of funds will be acceptable as payment for charges. In general, certified checks, bank checks and cash are the only acceptable ways to pay for a home.

Of course, every person named in the contract must sign the agreement.

While a contract that included only this information would certainly be legally binding, it would also be absurdly open-ended. It could lead to all manner of disagreements and problems. Accordingly, other clauses should be included in the contract.

This is your attorney's chance to shine. Studying, analyzing and rewriting the contract is the most important part of your attorney's role in the real estate purchase. The majority of his billable work will take place after the price has been agreed to and before you go to title. It is here that hiring an astute, experienced pro will pay off. The average attorney doesn't even read the form contracts. He probably has a rider he stole from someone else and attaches it to every real estate contract. That's why yours isn't the average attorney. The experienced real estate pro has come by his knowledge not from law school, which doesn't teach the first thing about these kinds of deals, but from the school of hard knocks. He learned by trial and error, through the raw stuff of first-hand experience. And since he's an old pro, he won't be learning his lesson on your home contract.

A good lawyer will be sure to add a series of clauses to protect your interests. Below are a few of the most important. If your lawyer doesn't raise these issues, you should.

The first item in the contract which your attorney should insist on customizing is the mortgage contingency clause. If you are financing any part of the purchase price, you should have written into the contract a provision which dictates the length of the mortgage you are willing to take, and the maximum interest rate that you would be willing to accept. Without these contingencies, you may be forced to accept any mortgage, whatever the terms, or else lose your deposit. Make sure that a particular rate is specified. Make sure the contract says no more than that the mortgage should be at the "prevailing rate." This mortgage contingency clause should also state the cutoff date for you to get bank approval. In most cases, you'll be able to get extensions, but try to ensure that you have more than enough time. (Also be sure to find out from your bank how long it takes to process a mortgage application. Depending on the housing market, it could take anywhere from three weeks to two months.)

Hopefully you'll have followed my advice, and will have already had the home inspected during the negotiation process. If you haven't—or if the broker talked you into using an inspector who was tucked away in his hip pocket—make sure there is a clause in the contract allowing you to have your own engineer inspect the property and report to you any defects or problems. Check to see that you have an exit in case any structural deficiencies should be uncovered. Make sure there is also a clause allowing you to have the home inspected for termites, insects and other pests. Also make sure it permits you to walk away if they are found.

Don't settle for a clause that gives you only the right to take back your deposit if the title proves to be faulty. Make sure that here, and in all other cases of seller's default, you are entitled to have your legal fees paid, as well as any other expenses you've incurred. You don't want to pay for the title search that turned up the liens on the seller. If any title problem can be cured by the payment of monies up to $1,000, the seller should be forced to do so.

Your real estate contract should include clauses that specify the form of ownership you will be taking: individual, joint tenancy or tenancy in common. Spouses usually opt for joint tenancy, which ensures that a surviving partner will inherit ownership. In a tenancy in common ownership arrangement, ownership passes to the heirs in case of the death of one partner.

The contract will spell out exactly how much of a deposit is due upon signing the contract, and of what the deposit should consist. The general practice is to put down 10 percent of the total purchase price in cash. Try not to fall victim to general practice however—10 percent is a lot of cash to lose if there is a default. The seller and his attorney will of course be looking for as large a deposit as possible, believing that the larger the deposit, the less likely you are to walk away from a deal. On the other hand, the buyer wants the lowest deposit possible. Here's a place for your attorney to show his mettle. Have him push for a figure lower than 10 percent, or negotiate to have the deposit include part cash and the balance by promissory note to conserve your cash, especially if this is a long-term contract. I've found that very often a seller will accept a deposit made up of 5 percent in cash and 5 percent in a promissory note.

This leads us to the next clause that should be included in the customized real estate contract: the structure of escrow agreements—who holds deposits and payments from the day they are doled out until title is transferred, and what types of accounts are created. First, the contract should stipulate that all escrow accounts are interest bearing. Make sure that attorneys or title company representatives, not brokers, are chosen to hold the monies. Since brokers have a financial interest in seeing the deal go through, they aren't impartial. In addition, they may not be licensed, which means they are accountable to no one. Let the seller's attorney hold the escrow. He's accountable—you know he isn't going to skip town with the cash, or use it to buy a new car. As for interest, make sure that the contract stipulates that the eventual recipient of the monies receive the interest. In the case of the deposit, for example, you would receive the interest if the deal fell through; if everything worked out, the seller would. Try to reach an agreement on the escrow arrangements before drawing up the contract. If you don't, you could spend a great deal of time and energy focusing on escrow terms, rather than contract terms.

It is possible for buyers to obtain the right to assign the contract to another party of their choosing before the closing. Often, buyers and their attorneys don't even bother to ask for it. Sometimes sellers' attorneys will write into the contract a clause that binds buyers' heirs to the agreement in the event the buyers die. It may be possible to trade the right of assignment for an agreement that does not bind your heirs. If you are buying a co-op or condo, try hard to keep that right of assignment. It may be worth a great deal of money to you if the building is in demand and prices are rising at meteoric rates. In general, however, the right to assign is a safety valve for the buyer in case disaster of one kind or another strikes, and closing becomes either impossible or undesirable.

Don't fall victim to lawyers, sellers or brokers who claim that it is "traditional" in their particular geographical area for the buyer to pay all the closing costs. Negotiate who will pay for what (i.e., in a rising mortgage market you may be able to get the seller to pay for some of your points), and have the terms written into the contract. Tradition shouldn't stand in the way of negotiation. Anything goes. God never made any rules about the sale of real estate.

Recently I represented a client who was buying property in Brooklyn. When I spoke to the seller's attorney about the contract, he noted that he would be including a possession clause that allowed the seller to remain as an occupant for a certain period of time after closing. I objected. He responded with "we always do it that way in Brooklyn." I told him we never do that in Manhattan, and refused to have it appear in the contract. Attorneys, brokers and sellers will try to use "tradition" as a device to get what they want. Don't let them.

One of the most important clauses in the contract is that which spells out what is personal property and what is affixed to the real estate being sold. As I pointed out earlier in this book, real estate is anything that is attached to the earth, or to the house. That should mean appliances that are attached to plumbing systems, and furniture that is built into walls. It should mean that, but it doesn't always. Anything not specifically listed as being part of the sale won't be there when you use your keys for the first time. Contracts should include a list of personal property that is included with the sale, and also a list of property that isn't included. Never assume that something is a fixture and will automatically be included with the sale of the home. Both parties should be well aware of exactly what they are selling and buying before they sit around the table at the closing.

A couple who recently became clients of mine learned a difficult lesson about the difference between real estate and personal property when they purchased their first home ten years ago. They fell in love with a magnificent home and eagerly went through the purchase process. They both couldn't wait to have a romantic candlelight dinner under the magnificent crystal chandelier in the dining room, and enjoy after-dinner drinks in front of their fireplace with its marble mantel. On the day of the closing they inspected the home and found that the chandelier had been replaced by two bare lightbulbs and the mantelpiece was nowhere to be found. Since they could be removed, they had been.

A good contract will also contain a clause that stipulates the seller's liability for any damage to the home resulting from hurricane, storm, wind, rain, flood or fire. Make sure that you will be able to receive the home in the condition it was in when the contract was signed. In general, most contracts stipulate that in case of irreparable damage, such as a fire, the buyer can walk away from the contract and retrieve his or her deposit. Even so, make sure you have a clause inserted that forces the seller to bring his insurance up to "replacement cost" for the home. Most people do not insure for replacement value (the actual amount it would cost to rebuild the home at today's prices). By forcing the seller to do so, you will make sure that the home you have decided to buy can be rebuilt, in the event of a fire.

Clauses should be included that force the seller to maintain the landscaping and walks as well as the home itself during the period before the closing. There should also be a provision that stipulates that the home be turned over in "broom-clean" condition. Broom-clean means that there is no garbage or trash around; it doesn't mean, however, you could eat off the floor.

Broom-clean also doesn't mean that the seller will have vacated by the closing. Insist that the contract indicate that the home will be vacant on the day of the closing. Getting rid of someone living in the home after title closing is very difficult, expensive and time consuming. Have your attorney add a clause to the contract which states that failure to vacate the property on time results in a per diem reduction of the purchase price. Figure the amount based on two-times hotel rates.

Make doubly sure that the contract allows for an inspection several days before the day of the closing by you or your designated agent to ensure that the home is in the condition agreed upon. Include another clause that allows another inspection on closing day itself. That several-day leeway gives the seller a chance to remedy problems, and eliminates any embarrassment you may have over raising problems at the closing table in front of your bank's attorney. Don't let the seller or his attorney convince you that he'll clear up the problems on the day of closing, or worse, thereafter. If there is a problem at the closing, the only way to ensure that it will be taken care of is to hold money out from the purchase price and place it in an escrow account until the work is done. Set a deadline; after it passes, you can get the monies from the escrow to take care of the problem yourself.

If you are purchasing a brand-new home from a developer, sponsor or builder, there are some other clauses that your attorney should make sure appear in the contract. Very often the sales agent for a new condo building or tract development will say that their contract is ironclad, and that they do not allow any changes. That's wrong. If the sales agent persists, have your attorney go directly to the sponsor or developer. If he, too, stubbornly refuses to negotiate the contract, find another home.

When negotiating the contract with a developer, builder or sponsor, stipulate that the plumbing, roof and other systems in the home should be guaranteed for at least a year after the title closing. The seller should also agree to return and make repairs should any problems arise. All subcontractor warranties and manufacturer guarantees on building materials used in the construction of the home should be turned over to you and not remain in the builder's hands. Your contract for the purchase of a new home should always include in it an outside date for closing and occupancy. New construction is often subject to extensive delays. For that reason, you should insist that the contract contain a provision that the seller will provide you with a duplicate mortgage if, due to these delays, your mortgage commitment expires and it becomes impossible to get a new one at the same or a lower rate. Make certain that, if you cannot close and take occupancy by a particular date, the deal is cancelled and your deposits, fees, charges and expenses are returned.

Remember that there is no maximum number of clauses or conditions that can be added to a contract. Make sure that every question you have, every worry you face, is dealt with in the contract. There are a thousand ways for a deal to fall apart between contract and closing. Every conceivable eventuality should be addressed in your agreement, and of course, each clause should be written so that it is as much to your advantage as possible.

Your attorney will hire his favorite title insurance company to investigate the title, looking for any problems. Generally, title problems arise through attorney error. That's why you are having an outside firm of title specialists handle the title search. The title company's searcher will read the prior deeds on the property, and will write a short history of the passage of title. The report will then be forwarded to the attorneys representing both sides. If there are any difficulties with the title, the seller's attorney should handle them. At the closing, another employee of the title company, the closer, will take care of all the paperwork generated by the purchase of the home. This includes the new mortgage, the satisfaction of an existing mortgage and the recording of the new deed.

I cannot implore you strongly enough to read the entire contract, word for word, and to ask your attorney to explain

each and every clause in detail. There are no stupid questions. After all, you are buying the home and signing the
agreement, not your attorney. Don't let him get away with
saying that a clause is "standard." Remember, yours is a
custom deal.

CHAPTER TWELVE

HOME FINANCING: A GUIDED TOUR OF THE MARKET

There's gold in them thar hills!
MARLENE DIETRICH IN
DESTRY RIDES AGAIN

It is the rare individual who has the financial resources to reach into savings and pull out enough cash to make a down payment on a home. Rarer still is the individual who—regardless of financial resources—should ever pay for a home in cash. I would go so far as to say that *no one*—neither the blue collar laborer nor the Fortune 500 executive—should pay for a home in cash. And that goes for people who are eighty years old as well as those twenty years old.

Leverage—the ability to spend a large sum of money today based on your potential to earn that money in the future—is perhaps the single most liberating tool of capitalism. It allows your investment in a down payment of, let's say $10,000, to grow and appreciate as if it had the power of $100,000—the total purchase price you paid for the home. (And the federal government shares in the cost of that leverage to the extent that your mortgage payments are tax deductible.) There is nothing wrong with borrowing to improve the quality and productivity of your life. And of all the reasons to borrow, none is more rewarding—personally as well as financially—than the purchase of a home.

Mortgages are powerful tools that enable you to do things that otherwise you would be incapable of doing. They are not burdens. They should be treated like any other monthly expense, not as a thirty-year ball and chain. Treat the mortgage obligation with all the respect you normally show for debts but with none of the fear. Look at a mortgage as an extremely benevolent silent partner in your home investment. And regard this partner as being the one who shares none of the profits, has no voice in your decisions, and is perfectly satisfied with the monthly payment you hand over.

By its very nature, the mortgage process allows us to get a leg up on the rest of our lives. We don't select a mortgage based on what we can afford this year, but rather what we will be able to afford over the next three to five years. Mortgages allow us to bet on our own future—and what could be a better gamble?

While there is a definite correlation between interest rates and affordability, rising rates should never lead you to postpone or—heaven forbid—abandon the hunt for a home. Don't panic when you hear that the prime lending rate is rising. A boost in interest rates only means that you have to shift directions a bit and perhaps take on a partner—the seller—who is likewise hurt by the change in the market. Remember: You can always buy a different, cheaper home when the cost of borrowing rises, but the seller has only one product for sale. He sees the demand for his product fall off with the change in the lending climate, and will be willing to reduce his price and/or give you help in the crucial matter of the financing.

The days are thankfully gone when consumers approached banks hat in hand, pleading their case for a mortgage. Banks benefit enormously from mortgage loans. They have discovered that home mortgages are the most secure, healthy and profitable investments open to them. In fact mortgages are so popular with financial institutions that those which don't deal with the general public actually go out of their way to purchase mortgages from urban consumer banks in order to get a piece of this profitable business. In today's mortgage market, a savvy middle-class buyer can march into a lending institution and be treated like a millionaire by pressing the right buttons with the bank officer. Today, banks are the supplicants.

I'll teach you how to find and press those buttons in Chapter Thirteen. But before we can master this process, it's important to understand what all those strange financial terms mean: exactly what a mortgage is, what it contains, where it comes from, and what various types of mortgage are available.

The *mortgagee* is the person or institution who lends the money. You, the borrower, are the *mortgagor. Principal* is the amount you are borrowing. *Interest* is the fee you pay to use someone else's money. The monthly payment, or debt service, is a combination of principal and interst. In fixed-rate mortgages, the amount of principal owed decreases as the years go on. Therefore the interest on it also declines, while the payment remains the same. In that way, home owners gradually reach a point where they are paying off the principal of the loan, rather than the interest. Called the "cross over," this usually occurs twelve to fifteen years into the loan term.

Owner's equity is the market value of the home, less the liens or obligations against it.

Amortization is the systematic repayment of borrowed money over a specified period of time.

Negative amortization is a growth in the principal due to the monthly payment on a loan being insufficient to pay the interest charge. This happens when the mortgage stipulates that interest will vary with market conditions, but the size of the payment is fixed during the term.

Loan-to-value ratio is the relationship between the bank's appraised value of the home and the amount of money they will loan for its purchase. No bank will lend 100 percent of the home's value. It wants to be your partner, not your benefactor. Each bank's loan-to-value ratio is a function of the amount of risk it will take on. The larger a percentage your down payment makes up, the less risk for the banker. In general, banks will never offer more than a 90 percent loan-to-value ratio, and at times it may be difficult to get the 90 percent without taking out mortgage insurance.

A *mortgage loan* is actually a combination of two documents: the promissory note, and either a mortgage or a deed of trust.

A *promissory note* is the agreement to repay the loan. It generally runs two pages and contains the details of the agreement, such as the total amount borrowed, the interest rate charged, the length of time the debt is to last, late payment penalties and any stipulation on paying off the debt earlier than the due date.

The second document included in the mortgage loan varies depending on your state's laws. In most states, real estate mortgage loans fall under what is called *lien theory,* and the second document is called, simply enough, the mortgage. In a handful of states—Alabama, Arkansas, California, Colorado, Delaware, Illinois, Mississippi, Missouri, Nevada, New Mexico, Tennessee, Texas, Utah, Virginia, West Virginia and the District of Columbia—real estate mortgage loans fall under *title theory,* and the second document is called a "deed of trust."

A *mortgage*, by definition, is any financial instrument in

which title to real estate is reserved as security for the payment of a debt.

In lien states, the lender receives a claim on the home as collateral security for the note. Lien theory is a bit better for borrowers, since the foreclosure process can take a long time—anywhere from three to nine months—making lenders that much more hesitant to foreclose. The mortgage stipulates that the borrower promises to pay back the loan, and, should he go into default, the lender may foreclose on the loan, having it sold at public auction, with the cash going toward repayment of the defaulted loan. First mortgage liens take priority over every other type of lien except federal tax liens. If a second mortgage was in effect, or if additional judgment liens were placed on the property, those creditors would have to wait in line for their money behind the original lender.

In title theory states, a *deed of trust* is the second document in the mortgage loan. In these states, title to the property is actually held by a third party—an escrow agent. Should the mortgagor default on the loan, all the mortgagee has to do is collect the title from the escrow agent. The deed will actually be in the name of the escrow agent. This holds a speed advantage for the lender, and makes it possible to foreclose in less than ninety days.

The differences, other than the speed of foreclosure, are really legalistic and administrative. Under both theories, mortgage loans result in the same thing—your ownership of a wonderful home and a profitable investment.

Almost all mortgages include certain standard provisions which may or may not be subject to negotiation.

The *estoppel clause* says that, upon request, the homeowner will provide a written statement acknowledging the amount he or she owes. This allows your lender to sell the mortgage without any difficulty, establishing exactly how much is owed on the loan.

The *defeasance clause* voids the loan agreement upon payment of the total amount owed.

The *subordination clause* forces any second liens on the property, such as the owner selling and taking back a mortgage, to be subordinate to the original mortgage.

Covenants are stipulations which require the borrower to keep the property in good condition, insure it against damage, pay taxes on it and in general, keep it in good repair.

The **acceleration clause** says that if the borrower doesn't live up to the covenants, then the entire debt becomes due. It is also used to require that the balance of the mortgage become due when the mortgagor sells the property, thus keeping the mortgage from being passed on or assumed by others.

Mortgage loans come with a series of one-time charges, which are often used as part of their particular marketing program to convince you to borrow from them, and not their competitor across the street. While most mortgage loans will have the same effective interest rate, this can be camouflaged by naming the components differently, and by requiring certain funds to be paid up front as one-time costs, instead of later as interest points. In general, loans with high up front charges will carry lower interest rates, and vice versa.

The **prepayment penalty** is expressed as a percentage of the principal and is charged if you pay the balance due before the expiration date of the loan. These penalties can be substantial for the first three to five years of the loan. During that early portion of the loan the bank hasn't yet made any real profit. Once the loan has become profitable for the bank, they will generally lessen prepayment penalties. Adjustable-rate mortgages are usually prepayable without any penalty.

Points are advance interest payments. Paying one point is equal to paying 1 percent of the principal. These are due up front at the closing, and generally appear when the mortgage market is tight. Sometimes they are used by banks which are going to turn around and sell mortgages on the secondary mortgage market. They will keep the points as their profit, and sell the rest of the mortgage to another bank. Points can also be a cosmetic gimmick to make interest rates appear lower, as noted earlier. Points involved in the purchase of a principle residence are tax deductible.

Often expressed as points, but really a separate charge, the **origination fee** is a one-time extraordinary charge for administration costs.

The **appraisal, legal and application fees** are one-time charges the bank will levy, usually at the closing.

A *balloon payment* is used in short-term loans. Only monthly payments of interest are required, but a large payment—often amounting to the entire principal—must be made at the end of the loan period. Once the balloon becomes due, the borrower either refinances or sells the property. Some lenders require that borrowers sign a commitment to permanently finance the loan with them once the balloon has come due. These large final payments are sometimes referred to as "bullets."

To ensure that your shopping isn't clouded by all this bank marketing, the federal government insists that all mortgage advertising include a reference to the *APR*, or *annual percentage rate*, which is the effective percentage you will be paying when interest, points and some other fees are figured together. By looking at APRs, you will be able to compare and contrast the real cost of any two mortgages.

Since mortgages are increasingly an important part of a bank's portfolio, a host of innovative, often enticing mortgage options have become available in the past few years. The days are long gone when the only choice a borrower had was between twenty-five- and thirty–year payouts. Today, a borrower can find a mortgage tailored to his or her individual situation and financial needs. You need to shop around.

The standard fixed-rate mortgages have been joined by variable rate mortgages with a host of options, such as renegotiable rate mortgages, graduated payment mortgages, graduated payment adjustable mortgages, and reverse annuity mortgages. And if you expand your search outside the traditional institutional lenders, you'll find a whole different set of options: Shared appreciation mortgages, and graduated payment mortgages are available. These are not worth discussing in this book, however, since they are local experiments that really haven't yet found their place in the larger market. The only important conceptual decision you have to make is whether to choose a fixed-rate mortgage or an adjustable-rate mortgage.

Fixed-rate mortgages are the old reliables that our parents and our parents' parents used when they entered the home-owning market. In an FRM the interest rate charge is fixed for the entire term of the mortgage, which traditionally runs fifteen, twenty-five or thirty years, depending on local traditions and regulations.

The obvious advantage of an FRM is that while your income is growing, your monthly payment remains the same, allowing you to develop equity within a relatively short period of time. In an adjustable-rate mortgage, it is possible that your monthly payment could keep rising along with your income. In addition, the fixed rate of interest offers stability in a market known for its fluctuations.

Locking in a mortgage at a low rate is certainly a plus, but it is also possible to lock in and watch rates plummet. Because of the volatility of interest rates, FRMs are becoming something of an endangered species today. Banks can be hurt by lending great amounts of money at fixed low rates for long periods of time and then seeing inflation push rates sky-high. To keep from falling into that trap (as many savings and loan associations did in the seventies), many financial institutions today shy away from FRMs. They are priced more dearly than adjustable rate mortgages because of this risk.

Many years ago, some innovative bankers in California and New England came up with a way to link mortgage interest rates to the fluctuations in the economy. They developed the *adjustable-rate mortgage,* in which interest rates rise and fall with market conditions; the size of your monthly payment is tied to an index used by the lender. The maximum increase in interest in one year will usually be limited to 1 or 2 percent. If market rates drop, the payment must be reduced accordingly. ARMs can usually be paid off without a prepayment penalty within ninety days after each change period. ARMs have boomed, particularly in times of double digit inflation.

Buyers and lenders both view ARMs as being especially well-suited to new home-owners who expect to spend a short period of time in their first home. The up-front points that have to be payed by the borrower at the closing are lower with an ARM than an FRM. Since, as we have previously discussed, most of us will own between three and five homes during the course of our lives, ARMs can provide an especially valuable alternative—particularly for those first two or three home purchases.

One interesting ARM option is a negative amortization feature, which allows the lender to add the increased cost of rising interest rates onto the unpaid principal of the loan, so that monthly payments remain fixed and are predictable. This is particularly advantageous for the first-time home owner operating on a tight budget. But keep in mind that under an ARM your total indebtedness can increase over time, cutting into your equity.

Because of their attractiveness to lenders, some real estate pundits predict that ARMs will become the standard type of mortgage loan in the future.

A third type off leverage that deserves consideration is **seller-assisted financing.** This arrangement can take any one of a thousand permutations. These could include the seller paying points for you, taking back a standing loan with or without interest, or taking back a second mortgage to blend with your new first, thereby letting you opt for a lower total on the first mortgage. The seller-assisted second loan can be invaluable in times of high interest rates.

While most sellers want their money up front and in one lump sum, there may be instances where providing you with a mortgage may be financially advantageous to them. Perhaps an elderly couple could use another source of regular income. Maybe a middle-aged seller could use the payoff to come in gradually, for tax purposes. It's up to you, your attorney and your accountant to come up with attractive proposals for the sellers. Don't expect them to become lenders on their own initiative.

You may also hear terms such as buy-down mortgage, assumable mortgage, and second mortgage bandied about while shopping. Let's look at what these expressions mean.

A *buy-down mortgage* is one in which the interest rate is below the current market rate, thanks to an entrepreneurial seller who has gone to a bank and made up the difference in income between the lower, more attractive rate, and the normal market rate. Generally this is done by developers of new tract housing projects and condominiums to attract purchasers when interest rates are high.

An *assumable mortgage* is one that allows the unfulfilled portion to be taken over by another party, as long as the obligations continue to be met. This would allow you to sell an attractive (i.e., low interest rate) mortgage along with your home, thus providing an important incentive to potential buyers. While this was avoided by banks for many years, it has now become popular again as another means to attract you to their product. It offers you the option of assigning their mortgage to someone else who might benefit from taking yours over instead of obtaining one of their own.

A *second mortgage* uses the equity built up in a home as the collateral for another loan. Generally these are used for home improvements or to draw needed cash out of the home investment.

In selecting a mortgage product to go after, there are a few things to keep in mind. The longer the mortgage term, the easier it is to qualify for. The lower the rate of interest on a mortgage, the easier it is to get. But as I said earlier, the key choice you have to make is between fixed-rate mortgage and an adjustable-rate mortgage.

I advise nearly everyone to get an adjustable-rate mortgage with the smallest monthly payment available. ARMs are, of course easier to obtain. Their payments are lower in the beginning, and usually increase as the years go on. This makes them especially appealing to younger buyers who may be stretching in the early years, and who in all probability will be selling before the payments get too high. I believe in playing the mortgage market, especially if you are young. With an ARM you are betting on your future—a perfect bet for a young person. And if you need the comfort of predictable monthly payments, you can get an ARM that has a negative amortization feature (i.e., fixed payment schedule).

Make no mistake, it *is* riskier to go with an ARM. But the risk factor, when compared to other investments, and when balanced with the advantages, is reasonable. If you are ambitious and upwardly mobile—no matter what your age—an adjustable-rate mortgage is for you.

The only clients I advise to get a fixed-rate mortgage are those—such as older couples—who will be living in the home for a long period of time, and to whom the predictability and stability of steady monthly payments are psychologically, as well as financially, important.

Whether you will pursue institutional or creative avenues for your financing to a very large extent depends on how ordinary or extraordinary your home purchase is. If you are making enough money for the average banker to readily approve the loan amount you are requesting, the institutional route will probably make the most sense.

There are several institutional sources for conventional home financing: mutual savings banks and savings and loan associations, commercial banks, credit unions, government agencies, finance companies, mortgage bankers and mortgage brokers. Let's examine these briefly.

Mutual savings banks and *savings and loan associations* were once the primary sources of home financing. But the financial jolts of the 1980s put many S & Ls out of business. Though times are better now, many savings banks are still a bit gun shy when it comes to mortgages—especially ones of the fixed-rate variety. Still, banking is a competitive business, and the home mortgage is potentially one of the most profitable and safest long-term loans a bank can make. You'll find that these institutions offer mortgage products, but they don't tout them as loudly as their commercial brethren.

Large *commercial banks*, which once upon a time concentrated on the big business customer, now look upon home mortgage loans as a prime source of stability and profit. They will often offer the most favorable terms and, in their competitive fervor, will be the most vocal about it.

Credit unions are expanding out of the second mortgage and home improvement loan categories and are trying to latch onto the profit that abounds in home mortgages. They may be an excellent source for qualified buyers to get prime lending terms.

Some *finance companies* are in the mortgage business, in addition to the home improvement, home equity and debt consolidation markets. While their terms may not be as attractive as commercial banks, they may not be as rigid in their screening.

Mortgage bankers do the legwork for large hybrid financial organizations, so that they can get involved in the mortgage market. By screening and qualifying applicants, finding loans, putting up the initial loan and then selling it to another lender or institution, mortgage bankers bring dollars from large businesses, such as insurance companies (which have neither the time nor the inclination to do the up-front work) into the home mortgage market. While mortgage bankers may eventually place your loan with another company, they will collect and manage the loan throughout its lifetime, charging the eventual mortgage holder a service fee.

In addition, large consumer finance companies (such as American Express and Sears Roebuck), brokerage houses and life insurance companies are all venturing into the mortgage business. Each day, it seems, another one enters the pack, all based on the theory that if they hold your mortgage they'll also be able to get involved in other profitable parts of your financial life.

Mortgage brokers really aren't sources of financing. Instead, they match up lenders and borrowers for a fee. If your financial situation is unusual, or money is tight, brokers can help you find a financial institution willing to give you a mortgage. They never provide the loan themselves, and in fact, their fee will be in addition to the standard fees and charges levied by the lender. But if you have a credit problem, they can be of great assistance. If you live in a large urban area, there may even be times when the mortgage broker, by being able to use his contacts outside your state, can find a lower interest rate than is available through local banks.

Now that you have some background in the various products available and their sources, it's time to begin the mortgage application process.

CHAPTER THIRTEEN

GETTING
A
MORTGAGE

Put money in thy purse. . . .
fill thy purse with money. . . .
Make all the money thou canst.
SHAKESPEARE (OTHELLO)

When a bank, or any other financial institution, considers lending you money, it is concerned with three things: your *willingness* to pay back the loan, your *ability* to pay the loan and the value of the *collateral* offered to secure the loan. Meet these three requirements and you'll get the loan.

Mortgagees ascertain this information in a number of ways. They judge your willingness to pay by examining your credit report, which has detailed information on your past and present credit experience, and they draw interesting (and sometimes dubious) conclusions from certain of your answers on the mortgage application. They gauge your ability to repay the debt by measuring the ratio of your monthly gross income to living expenses and other debt. The value of your collateral—in the case of a mortgage loan, the home you want to buy—is verified by an independent appraisal.

Despite the enormous fear and uncertainty surrounding this process, there is a mortgage loan and a mortgage lender for everyone. But to get that mortgage, you'll have to make sure that the mortgagee sees you and your financial life in the best possible light. Lies will not work and are unnecessary anyway. The only tools you will need are the truth and an understanding of the systems mortgagees use to make their decisions.

The first step in any type of credit transaction is to pre-check your credit report—the same report that bankers and other potential lenders will be examining when you make the application. And the time to begin correcting and "cleaning" your credit report is when you start searching for a home—long before the banker sees it. Mortgage bankers don't like surprises.

Contact TRW, Trans Union or whichever major credit bureau covers your area, and find out how to get a copy of your credit report or profile. You are entitled to it by law. If you have been denied credit within the past thirty days, you can obtain a copy at no charge. Otherwise, a copy of the report will cost anywhere from $5 to $15. Generally, to obtain the report, you will have to write a letter to the bureau requesting your report. In your letter you should include your full name, your current address (together with any others you have had within the past five years) and your Social Security number.

Once you receive your credit report, study the accompanying explanation of the codes used in the report. While most credit reports are fairly straightforward, they are intended for use by grantors of credit, not consumers, and therefore can be a bit complicated to interpret.

Each line in the report—called a "trade line"—details either a request for information about your credit or an action taken by a grantor of credit regarding your account with them. Each credit grantor will often qualify your status with them through the use of a code.

There are two major types of codes. TRW uses the terms POS, NON and NEG. POS means that your account is current and that you have paid all your bills on time or before 60 days. NON means that your status is nonevaluated—a neutral term meaning that your account may be sixty days late or more, but less than ninety days late. The NEG rating is reserved for accounts that are ninety days late or more, and for bankruptcies, charge-offs, tax liens, judgments settled and other negative situations. Trans Union's qualifying system uses a scale of numbers from 1 through 9. Number 1 means that bills are consistently paid on time, while numbers 7, 8 and 9 represent different stages of delinquency or default.

Remember: The grantors of credit decide on this qualification not the credit bureau. One department store might assign you a NON rating after paying late only once in the course of a year. Another store might not remove you from the POS position until you have been late three or four times in the same period.

A clerk in the bank, not the banker himself, will be checking this credit report. Usually, they will scan the column and look for some overall trend in your other credit grantors' feelings about you. A series of NON and NEG ratings will immediately place you in the "loan application denied" pile. Sometimes, a single NEG can keep you from getting a loan. In the view of most banks, a lack of credit experience reflects negatively on your credit status.

Examine your report with all the diligence of a proofreader. Credit bureaus are notorious for printing embarrassing errors. I don't intend to apologize for these nearly invisible "big brothers." Yet they are responsible for gathering billions of pieces of information on millions of people. Mistakes are inevitable. And the appearance of information—correct or not—on a computer-printed credit report automatically lends to it a ring of truth. It could in fact refer to something that happened five years ago, but it nevertheless looks like today's news. None of this information should be considered factual until it has been verified by you—the person it most affects.

If you discover an error in your credit report, send a letter immediately to the bureau outlining your discovery. State that you want the bureau to verify the information and delete it if it cannot be substantiated. Keep a copy of that letter. Credit bureaus are required by law to investigate and eliminate errors in a timely fashion. Despite their uncaring reputations, they are in the business of selling accurate information, and want to make sure that their data is correct. If they can obtain no confirmation, the trade line in question must be deleted. Major credit bureaus allocate fifteen business days to substantiate entries. If within that time they can't back up the information, they will remove it from your file. Since the burden of proof is on them to prove their statements, you should not be timid in challenging any entry you find questionable. Enclose, if you wish, any pertinent materials that corroborate your claims. Make sure to send copies of documents, not the originals. Attach another copy of the correspondence to an extra copy of the credit report. If the changes you have pushed for don't show up on the report by the time it gets into the bank's hand, you'll want to indicate that you have taken certain specific actions to clear up your credit file. Sometimes, the mere evidence that you have taken positive steps toward resolving credit deficiencies is enough to satisfy a loan officer.

Facts are often perceptions. Sometimes, the terminology used by grantors can be changed if you offer legitimate reasons for slow payment, and document them. Press the grantor, not the credit bureau, for the correction and/or elimination of any negative wordings that may appear on your report. Catch up with your payments and pay back balances, certainly, but also make sure that the grantor in turn sends notification to the credit bureau to change your status or code.

When one client of mine prechecked his credit report, he found that Bloomingdales had labeled him as a "slow pay" for being ninety days late in paying a bill. He went directly to the store and confronted the manager of the credit department. He advised her that he had bought a set of dishes and had them sent to his summer home. When he opened the box, he discovered that they were broken. He called the store and a sales clerk told him she would take care of the problem and that he shouldn't pay the bill until the replacements arrived. The new, unbroken set of dishes arrived at his summer home ninety days later, at which time he paid the bill. In fact, he did pay slowly, but he was justified in doing so. He left the store with a letter from the store's credit manager instructing the credit bureau to remove the "slow pay" label.

If, after making corrections and attempting to have grantors' negative judgments changed, your credit report still has an overall negative or ambiguous tone, or contains a sequence of negative events—not truly representative of your current condition, but perhaps a litany of past misdeeds—it will be necessary for you to address and correct this interpretation.

By law you are allowed to have a one hundred–word consumer statement added to your credit report to clarify entries such as a rash of late payments, tax liens, and/or judgments that might have occurred during an extraordinary period of your life—such as a divorce proceeding, for example. The letter can balance out negative statements with explanations that put the event into context. For example, a slow payment record in 1980 can be countered with an explanation that a prolonged bout with hepatitis brought about a short-term cash shortage, causing the late payments, which eventually were all met. In your statement you can show that you have attempted to cure problems—for example, that you are paying back due amounts, or are in the process of paying double monthly payments—in order to clear up your credit report.

Request that the consumer statement become a permanent part of your credit report, not just a footnote. Credit bureaus are apt simply to note the availability of such a statement. But the law stipulates that at your request, they have to include it with every report.

A consumer statement clarifying the negative tone of a report does wonders for your standing in the eyes of a sophisticated credit grantor, because it demonstrates that you care about your credit, which is in itself an important element in credit worthiness.

With your credit history sanitized and beautified for grantor consumption, the next step in the process is to hunt for a bank—one that offers the mortgage you are looking for and that cares to work for you.

While most banks eventually catch up with one another and offer the same rates, there may be a period when one "takes the lead" and the others haven't yet caught up. Comparison shopping is worthwhile, since it's possible for you to find the current rate leader. In addition, some banks have more generous loan-to-value and -income ratios, making their products more available to you.

Remember, before you start chasing down potential lenders, you should have settled on a particular mortgage product in order to make valid comparisons between the banks' offerings. There is no reason why you can't change your mind later in the process, but to shop for comparisons most effectively, you need at least to settle temporarily on a mortgage type.

Compile a list of all the financial institutions in your area that offer mortgages; include all the savings and loans, saving banks, commercial banks, mortgage bankers, responsible finance companies, credit unions, as well as "new players" like insurance companies and credit card companies. Check the yellow pages to see if there is a mortgage compilation service in your area. These organizations compile lists of lenders and the mortgage products they are offering, making comparisons less difficult.

Then call each institution, introduce yourself as a potential customer, and ask to speak to a loan officer about home mortgages. You should have no problem getting through to someone—after all, banks are in the business of lending money, and home mortgages are their favorite products.

Once you get the loan officer on the phone, be pleasant. You need to gather a tremendous amount of information in this first contact with the bank and you don't want to be cut off in any way. You have to get answers to all your questions—answers you understand.

First, ask about the fixed-rate mortgages being offered by the bank. For each product offered, find out what the interest rate is; how long the term is; what the aggregate points are, if any; and what the annual percentage rate (APR) is.

Next, find out what types of adjustable-rate mortgages the bank is offering. For each offering, find out what the rate is; how long the terms are; what the points are, if any; what the change period is; what the maximum allowable change is for each period, and over the life of the loan; whether or not the loan can be converted to a fixed-rate instrument in the future without additional expenses; and what index is used as a basis in adjusting the rate.

Ask the loan officer what the bank's minimum down payment requirements are. Find out if there is a maximum loan amount and what it is. Check to see if the nature of the dwelling—apartment, single-family or two-family home—affects the rate charged. Ask how long it will take for the bank to approve your loan application.

In your conversation with the loan officer, discuss the bank's loan-to-value ratio requirement and -income ratio (the maximum percentage of monthly gross income it believes someone should allocate for shelter). Some banks remain bound to tradition and insist that no more than 25 percent of your gross monthly income should go toward shelter. Others keep pace with changing costs that have raised the ceiling to 30 percent. There is no reason for the bank to be secretive about these ratios. If the loan officer refuses to disclose the numbers, ask to speak to his or her supervisor. If you still get no satisfactory answer, find another bank.

These ratios are usually based on two theories. The first is a straight income-to-housing cost formula. Here the lender computes your anticipated housing costs, including the mortgage payment, real estate taxes, insurance, maintenance (for co-ops) and common charges (for condos). The lender will usually use a 25 percent calculation. This means that these monthly housing expenses cannot exceed 25 percent of the applicant's gross monthly income.

The other most popular (and generally used) method computes your anticipated housing expenses and adds to them all of the applicant's debt payments. Included in these expenses are car payments, charge account payments, child support and alimony payments, other real estate loans, overdraft checking accounts, personal loans and student loans. Debts that will be paid off at or prior to the closing or that will expire ten months after mortgage disbursement or less will not be included in the bank's debt computation.

I have seen a range of percentages used by banks in computing this ratio that run anywhere from 28 percent to 36 percent, depending on factors such as the particular bank's underwriting policies or whether there is private mortgage insurance. Ratios, of course, can be overridden by senior underwriters at many institutions.

Now you can see why the longer the term of the loan and the lower the interest rate, the more the bank will lend.

Ask what the total amount of all fees come to—including appraisal, bank attorney, credit check and application. Find out if the bank's loans carry any prepayment penalties, what they are and when they occur.

Check with the loan officer about the special programs that the bank offers to prior customers. See if the bank has other programs that can speed up the decision-making process, such as no income-verification loans.

Find out the bank's mortgage commitment policies regarding how long the commitment is good for; also if renewals are available and at what rate. If the closing is postponed unavoidably, will the commitment vanish? Ask whether or not the bank locks in the interest rate at the time of application (or at the time of commitment), or if it remains variable until you sign the final documents at the closing. Some banks will want to write the loan at the prevailing interest rate at the time of closing, not application. Others will work for you, cutting the rate if the market should drop, but holding it steady should the market rise. Ask if you will have to pay any charges at the time of the commitment.

After you have polled the banks on your list, asked all the

questions, compared the answers and decided which bank and which product are the best for you, it's time to pick up an application, take it home and fill it out with a great deal of care.

Almost all mortgage applications look alike. They are designed to determine both your *ability* and your *willingness* to pay back the loan. These questionnaires seem extremely complicated. They want to know: your gross salary; your current address; whether you own the property or rent; the length of time you have been living there; any other addresses you have lived at in the past five years; a listing of all your assets, including your bank accounts; and all of your obligations. There is a good reason for their complexity—good in the bank's eyes anyway. They are using this application as another means of judging your character—your willingness to pay—not just your financial ability to pay.

This analysis, based upon scoring systems, assigns a numeric value to the answers you give on the application. The bank has looked at customers who have defaulted, at customers who have fulfilled their obligations. As a result, it has come up with a series of traits or characteristics which it believes must be present for a borrower to be a safe, secure mortgagor. It then asks questions to find out if the applicant does in fact have those traits. Each response is given a score indicative of how close to the perfectly safe answer it comes. To get a mortgage loan an applicant has to score above a certain total. Otherwise, he or she is deemed to be a poor risk.

In the good old days, loan officers would sit down and interview prospective borrowers in order to determine their character—their willingness to pay. But it was deemed too expensive to continue this interview process. Instead, scoring was put in its place. That way, a clerk could qualify mortgage applicants, freeing the higher-paid loan officer to do other, "more important" work. The IRS uses similar scoring systems to determine who will be audited.

The interview process may have been more intimidating than the form application, but at least it afforded to the prospective mortgagor a chance to explain aspects of his or her life that might seem untoward. The application, on the other hand, asks direct questions and leaves only enough room for straightforward, to the point answers. The applicant is given no opportunity to explain an answer, thus leaving him at the mercy of a lower echelon clerk and a list of numeric codes that totally depersonalize the lending process.

But there is a way to beat the system, to bypass the clerks and the scoring system, and to restore some humanity and individuality to the process. The trick is to turn the application into a window on your life.

The answers that are worth the most points in your score are those which reflect the highest degree of stability and security. If there is any possible answer to give to a question on the application which in any way might reflect poorly on your stability, implying (at least to the bank) that you are a high risk for a mortgage loan, don't simply fill in the blank. Instead, fill in a note or asterisk referring the reader to a supplement you have attached. In that supplement, explain and rationalize your answer, couching it in the most positive terms.

The bank also uses mathematics to determine your ability to pay back a loan. It takes the income ratios which it loves so dearly and applies them, based on your answers to the application's limited questions. If the numbers that you have to give are likely to yield an inadequate ratio, it's time to draw up a supplement.

Let me go over with you some typical application questions and show you how a supplement can put your stability and income in a better light, making you appear more willing and better able to pay in the bank's eyes.

Answers to questions about your current residence are important measures of stability for the banker. Banks prefer home owners to renters, and the longer you have lived in the same place the better. Living in a motel or a furnished room is a definite no-no. Supplement your answer here by noting that while you have resided in a new apartment every year for the past four years, each has been a step up. Note either that they have all been in the same general area, or that career advancement has forced you to move frequently. Stress that changes in your residence have reflected growth, not instability.

If you have worked less than three years at your current job, banks will question your stability. Turn this around by supplementing your answer with a list of previous jobs and/or school attendance that shows that you have steadily advanced in your career and salary with each job move.

Any other question that looks to determine the length of time you have done something, or the degree to which you have changed course in your life, should be answered with a supplement, if there is any chance that your answer is open to a negative interpretation.

Employment questions are also important ingredients in measuring your ability to pay. When a bank asks for your monthly gross income, all it expects to see is a copy of your W-2 form from last year, a couple of pay stubs or sometimes your federal tax return. Accordingly, banks always have an easier time dealing with employees than self-employed individuals.

While a 1040 form may help establish the income credibility of a self-employed person, it will also, by its very nature, downplay income. Instead, you may have to supplement your 1040 with a profit and loss statement, or a letter prepared by your accountant. Detail any long-term contracts and business arrangements that make your self-employment more stable.

The "other income" section of a mortgage loan application is extremely important if you are having difficulty showing the income which the bank is looking for. It too leaves very little room for answers. Provide a supplement to this section, indicating interest from savings accounts, income from securities and other financial instruments, rents received, annual cash gifts—including those from relatives—cash settlements from litigation and any payments to you, either one time or recurring. Make sure you include monies derived from reasonable expectations, such as regular periodic salary raises, annual bonuses, perennial gifts, and debt repayments. (Include the termination date of recurring expenses, such as the end of a college loan payout. The cessation of a steady expense is actually an addition to your income.) Anything you can add and document to the "other income" section will greatly help your case, since it gives the intelligent loan officer a chance to consider your future earnings as part of the total income picture.

If all of this work still leaves you short of the bank's ratios—because your income is marginal or you are self-employed and lack sufficient documentation to demonstrate your income—you still have an option. Some banks offer nonverification mortgage loans in which your willingness to pay (credit history) is checked, but your ability to pay (income ratio) is not. Generally, the bank will offer no more than 75 percent as the loan-to-value ratio of these loans. But if that's your only chance, then go for it.

To help your customized application wend its way successfully through the red tape at the bank, it always helps to find a bank employee to act as a "shepherd" for it. Put on a suit and visit the bank with your application package in hand. Ask to speak to someone in the loan department.

In your warmest, most caring manner, tell the contact you meet that yours is a special mortgage application, and you have worked very hard on it. Show them the supplements you have attached, together with your credit file and the documentation of your efforts to "cleanse" it. Indicate the care with which you have filled out the application form and ask your contact to please keep a careful watch over your application as it wends its way through the bank's bureaucracy.

If your shepherd attaches a face and a personality to that application package, then you'll have gone a long way toward ensuring that you will get the fairest treatment possible. Contact your shepherd when or if you have any questions, and use these phone calls to check on the status of your loan application, reminding him or her of your concern and care.

If all has gone according to plan, you should have your commitment papers within three to five weeks.

But if something goes wrong and you find that your application has been rejected, don't give up. Rejection is not necessarily the end of the process. It's really just an immediate reaction to your application and credit report, not a permanent judgment that you aren't qualified to own a home and receive a mortgage.

By federal law, any mortgage loan rejection must give a

reason for the decision—the single factor that tilted the scales against you. Once you know the reason for your rejection, you can concentrate your efforts on clearing up that one specific problem. The appeal of a mortgage decision is one of the easiest to undertake, since you waste no time in finding out what went wrong—the bank has to tell you. Furthermore, the last thing the bank wants to do is deny you a mortgage. It actually costs them more to deny the mortgage application than to accept it. Rejections simply aren't cost-effective.

Call the loan department in the bank and find out exactly what the appeals process is. If one is in place, follow it meticulously to the letter. More than ever before, you now want to reinforce the impression that you are a responsible, stable individual.

If there is no established appeals process, then you'll have to create one of your own. Call the head of the bank's mortgage division and set up a meeting. Go as high as you have to. Don't be confrontational. Instead, enlist the officer as your ally. You know that you have the capacity to pay back the loan, the character to pay back on time and the collateral to give the grantor an exit. But obviously your application failed to make all that clear to the bank. Note: Never tell the banker he was wrong. Merely ask for reconsideration based on new or clarified facts.

Impress the lender with your concern. Indicate that you understand the bank's need for protection, but reemphasize your creditworthiness. Be persistent. The more contacts you make, the more chances you have to make a dent in that impersonal wall of bureaucracy. Supply the bank with new supplements and reworked applications. If you have to show additional income, bring in a guarantor—a relative or affluent friend—or get a part-time job. Schedule meetings with as many officers and officials as you can, and press the "up" button—speaking to superiors—whenever you get no satisfaction. There are hundreds of examples where persistence paid off and a negative decision was reversed.

At the same time you are pursuing this appeal process, go back to your phone notes and begin the application process at another bank. Don't put all your eggs in one basket, hoping to reverse the rejection. Work other avenues. And don't let a rejection sour you on the process. It was your application that was rejected, not you. There is a mortgage product and a mortgagee for everyone. It's simply a matter of finding the right one.

But in all likelihood, you'll never have to deal with the appeals process. Because by cleaning up your credit report, finding the best bank for you, expertly completing and supplementing the application to get the better of scoring, and finding a shepherd, you'll receive your commitment.

Once you receive this commitment, make a photocopy of it and send it to your attorney. Review it carefully with him, making sure that it matches the description given to you over the phone when you first contacted the bank. If there are any discrepancies, call the bank. If there is anything you don't understand, ask the attorney. If he doesn't know, have him call the bank. Commitments are somewhat negotiable. If there is anything that you or your attorney would like to change, discuss it with the bank. Only when you are absolutely satisfied with the terms of the commitment, and completely aware of all its conditions, should you sign and return it to the bank. A signed commitment is a binding contract. This will be your last chance to negotiate with the bank.

You are almost there. The light at the end of the tunnel— the glow of home ownership—is visible. The hard part is over. But you're not completely out of the woods. You still have to make it through the closing.

CHAPTER FOURTEEN

CLOSING
AND THE
PASSAGE
OF TITLE

I am monarch of all I survey.
WILLIAM COWPER

The *passage of title* is called different things in different parts of the country—"title closing" in the east and "settlement" in the west—and is generally an automatic, by-the-numbers process. Still, it's important to know what is going on and why. Buyers never receive anything at the closing that isn't stipulated in the contract. But it is possible to get short-changed.

This mechanical system is not equipped to deal with emergencies. And any problem that comes up at the closing is an emergency, requiring the attorneys for both sides to do some quick legal work. But many times the attorneys, believing the closing would be a mere formality, have paralegals representing them, or worse, delegate the whole system to an escrow company. Some states have regulations that make closings automatic as long as attorneys aren't involved; and brokers in those states will push hard to make this come about. Don't let it happen. You need a closing and you need an attorney, regardless of what the seller and broker say is common practice.

The most important thing to realize about the closing is its relative unimportance. Everything that goes on at the closing has been agreed to in the contract that we discussed in Chapter Eleven. Still, the closing is complicated and more than a bit intimidating.

Sitting around the table in the bank attorney's office you will be simultaneously borrowing money from the bank, passing it on to the seller, receiving a deed to the home, and finally, taking care of any last minute adjustments or snags.

There will be quite a crowd at the closing. Present will be you and the seller, the attorneys for both sides, your banker and/or your bank's counsel, the seller's banker if he is paying off a mortgage, the title company's representative, the broker, the managing agent's representative if the home is a co-op or condo and perhaps a creditor or two who may have liens against the property. They all will be stone-faced and solemn—not because the occasion is so inspiring, but because they are bored. The only people excited by the process are you and the seller. And the seller just wants to get out of there as soon as possible, check in hand. All of them see the closing as a routine process. Routine it may be, but care must be taken nevertheless.

I've seen closings where more than fifty checks changed hands. In fact, the number of checks that a buyer has to write at a closing has become part of American mythology. It is vital that you know exactly what you are spending and why, not just for peace of mind, but for your tax return next year. In America, closing costs typically run from 4 to 8 percent of the total purchase price, not including adjustments for local property taxes.

Uncle Sam has come around and agreed that there is need for a more comprehensive closing process. Banks are now required by law to provide you with a RESPA (Real Estate Settlement Procedures Act) statement which itemizes and summarizes the proceedings. But as often happens with government attempts at simplification, this has only resulted in more complexity. RESPA statements are impossible to decipher—for attorneys as well as consumers—and they are prepared at the closing, so they are not a map for what is going to happen.

I offer a pre-closing to my clients a few days before the actual event to familiarize them with the process and to make sure they are informed and prepared—in short, to demystify the process.

See if your attorney will do the same thing. Sit down with him prior to the closing, and have him run through the process, step by step, check by check. Have him find out exactly what every charge will be, or at least what the majority of them will be. In cases such as the attorney's own bill, where estimates are all you can hope for, get a high and low figure from the attorney. The attorney should explain every charge and fee, including the adjustments which I will discuss with you a little later in this chapter. He should have copies of all the documents you will have to sign, so you can at least read them at your leisure days before the closing. It's tough to read a mortgage with twenty eyes staring at you and the bank's attorney drumming his pencil on the table impatiently. And if there are any problems with the bank's documents, you'll have to deal with them before the closing itself. All a bank's attorney can do at a closing is hand you documents. He cannot make changes without first consulting his superiors.

Draw the checks beforehand. Find out which have to be certified checks and which can come from your personal account. Some attorneys for sellers will insist that even your certified checks and bank checks be drawn on local banks so that the seller can make use of the funds immediately, and won't have to wait five days for the out-of-town check to clear. If you don't know the exact amount of a charge, fill in the rest of the check. Clip a note to each check that says exactly what it is in payment for. Place in your briefcase the checks, a copy of the reconciliation statement, a copy of the contract, your insurance policies, a copy of your loan commitment letter, identification (such as a passport or driver's license), and your rabbit's foot. The more prepared and organized you are, the smoother the closing will go. If you are surprised by anything that happens at the closing, your attorney didn't do his job well.

It is traditional for your attorney to slip his bill in front of you at the closing and jokingly say "and while you're writing checks you might as well write one for this." Of course you'll be too busy (and perhaps a little embarrassed) to look at the bill, so you simply write another check. Don't do it. Tell your attorney that you'd like to pay him, or at least see a bill, a day or two before the closing. Let him estimate the hours at the closing and take care of any discrepancy later on.

Adjustments are payments you will be making to the seller for supplies and/or expenses that he has paid for which you will benefit from, or vice versa. They may also be called prorations. The fuel oil remaining in the tank, or the property taxes paid last month, for example. Often, these adjustments can be the last stumbling block in a difficult negotiation. Rules governing the calculation of adjustments vary from state to state. It's better to leave them to the pros on both sides and not let them get in the way of the exchange of title.

Attorneys would actually rather not have to do these calculations on the spot. I know from personal experience that it isn't easy to figure out an adjustment. You have to take the amount paid, let's say in April, for taxes through June, and figure out how much taxes cost each day. Then you have to calculate how much of the total payment should be allocated for the period from April until May 13 at midnight, the eve of the closing. You have to translate calculations based on fiscal years to calendar years. Taxes which are paid in advance and taxes which are paid late both have to be analyzed. As I said, it's not easy. Anyway, if the calculations are made and agreed to before the closing, you can already have the checks made out when you come to the closing table.

Adjustments aren't the only problems that could come up during closing. Anything that happens inconsistent with the terms of the contract is a problem. And these problems are serious because the moment title changes hands the contract ceases to exist and has no value at all. If anything is wrong and you still proceed to close, the seller is under no obligation at all to fix it. Forget about promises to take care of it in a day or two. The only workable agreements that survive the closing are those that are backed up by financial incentives or penalties.

If your final inspection reveals that furniture hasn't been removed, let your attorney know about it. It could cost you hundreds of dollars to remove furniture or garbage the seller should have removed. If the seller says that he'd like to stay on a couple of days more, slam on the brakes. If you agree to this, you might have to remove him physically, or worse yet, get a court order and have a marshall do it. In some states you would have to get an ejectment—a process that could take two years. Sellers who wish to stay on a while can be a major problem. Have your attorney draw up a possession agreement and make sure that in lieu of rent you have a per diem reduction in the purchase price. In the case of any other last minute problems, have your attorney draw up an agreement requiring the seller to take care of it and place money from your purchase price in escrow. Either attorney can hold the escrow account, but make sure that it is an interest-bearing instrument, and that the eventual recipient receives the interest.

Make sure that your final inspection, which should take place immediately before the closing, is done with a fine-tooth comb. Check every nook and cranny for latent problems. Many times buyers unearth serious conditions once the furniture and fixtures have been removed from the home. Don't hesitate to bring these problems to the seller's attention.

You might feel awkward raising any red flags at this point. After all, everyone is there, including your banker, and what difference does a little leak make? But don't back down. You still have a tremendous amount of power. The seller is almost always more afraid of not closing than you are. They may have to close on their new home tomorrow. The funds you are paying could be leaving their hands quite quickly, and any delay may seriously complicate their lives. Use this power. Closings can be a weapon that a savvy buyer and his attorney can wield effectively to resolve any last minute problems in his favor.

Let's take a brief look at all the fees and charges that have to be paid at closing. One note though: Nothing says that these have to be paid by the buyer. Your contract can stipulate that the seller is responsible for some, or even all of these costs. Remember, yours is a custom purchase.

Firstly, and looming largest, is your payment of the balance of the purchase price. You will probably be signing a bank check over to the seller after having signed your mortgage agreement.

But before the bank's lawyer hands you the big check, he's going to get from you a whole series of smaller, but not insubstantial checks. Mortgage costs can, and most often do, include payment of the points, an origination fee, an application fee, an appraisal charge, the bank's own attorney fees and the charge for the bank's title insurance protecting them from any title problems with the home. But the bank doesn't stop there. While part of your mortgage payment each month will consist of funds earmarked for taxes and insurance, the bank may not have enough to pay a six-month bill, since you have only been in the home three months. To further protect themselves, they will take from you an escrow advance to ensure that they have enough funds to cover a large bill coming due. Don't be overly concerned about this additional charge—the adjustments you make with the seller will cover them.

If your mortgage provides for negative amortization—as

many adjustable-rate instruments do—wherein monthly payments remain the same but the interest fluctuates—you will find some surprises cropping up in the bank's charges. Since the size of the mortgage may change from year to year, the bank will try to protect its lien position by increasing the amount of the principal, which will in turn increase other bank charges, such as the bank's mortgage insurance, which are keyed to the size of the principal.

If you are buying a co-op, there is another set of fees including credit investigation, processing and application charges that must be paid to the building's managing agent. Condos may require you to pay a month's worth of the common charges as an additional security deposit. Many apartment buildings, whether co-op or condo, will ask for deposits to move in—just in case you scratch the banisters or dent the elevator door. In some states you may have to pay a mortgage tax of from ¾ of 1 percent up to 2 percent of the total mortgage.

While you, as the buyer, are considered responsible for the mortgage tax, the seller has obligations as well. States have real estate transfer taxes and documentary taxes—called *stamps*—as well as land bank taxes, for which the seller is responsible. And just as you may be negotiating for the seller to pick up some of your costs, the seller may be pushing for you to take over his obligations. This is especially true when you are contracting to purchase a condominium or tract development home.

The title insurance company will also present you with a series of charges in addition to the insurance fee, including title search, building department and municipal agency search, survey inspection, recording and transfer fees. The recording charges are based on the size of the document being recorded and run from $2 to $5 per page. A mortgage may run anywhere from three to twenty pages, while a deed is usually no more than two pages. Condo deeds, though, often stretch to five pages. Good legal craftsmen will keep pages to a minimum. Title companies might also charge you an added fee if you have a variable rate mortgage.

The broker's commission, if any is due, is payable at the

closing. In a co-op transaction there may be a flip tax—an extraordinary fee charged by co-op corporations to enhance their financial reserves—due at the closing.

Bring a checklist of things that have to be picked up from the seller at the closing. Your list should include: the certificate of occupancy; any Underwriters Laboratory certificates for the home; permits for amenities such as pools, docks and tennis courts; and keys to the association's gym lockers or the condo's clubhouse.

Of course, don't forget to get the keys to all the doors from the seller. At this point the broker will probably give you a bottle of champagne and a basket of fruit. Enjoy them both. Rest assured, you've paid for them somewhere along the way.

Have a sip of champagne. Thank your attorney and everyone present. Get into your car and drive to your new home. Take a deep breath. Put the key in the lock. Open the door. Look around. This is *your home:* The whole process has been leading up to this moment, and there's nothing quite like it.

HOME
BUYING
FOR
OLDER
AMERICANS

I firmly believe that retirement is a nonevent. No one should ever stop doing things. Instead, when they feel ready, they should begin to do different things—less strenuous maybe, less nerve-racking certainly, but less important? Never. Whether you or your parents leave the job market because of company policy, or personal choice, it needn't spell an end to activity and usefulness. It may well, however, require a rethinking of your shelter needs.

Perhaps your parents' present home is too big for their needs. Maybe the costs associated with a large home can no longer be handled on a reduced retirement income. It's possible that the climate where they now live is too cold. City life may now seem too fast paced and no longer hold the advantages—such as proximity to work—it once did. Whatever the reason, older Americans make up an increasingly large percentage of the home-buying market.

But even though the reasons to buy are different, older Americans can generally follow all the rules we have laid out in this book. The blessings and problems of the last home you buy are exactly the same as the first home you buy. Retirees go through the same evaluations and steps that first home buyers do, with a few important exceptions.

The goals and priorities of older Americans are certainly going to be different from those of their children. Many rooms are no longer as important—dens and dining rooms for example. After all, entertaining may not be as frequent. Don't let your parents fall victim to the trap of buying a home with bedrooms for all their children—it's not necessary. Sure you'll come to visit, but you'll stay in a hotel. It's foolish for your parents to invest in a three-bedroom home just to make you more comfortable on your two yearly trips.

I have encouraged first-time home buyers to look at their purchase, not as the only home they will own, but as the first in a series of homes. On the other hand, older home buyers must look at their retirement home as the last home they will be buying. Because of this, location analysis takes on an even greater importance.

Your parents will be living in their retirement home for the remainder of their lives. Since areas won't be selected because of their proximity to work or schools, it becomes much harder to narrow the choices down. In fact, I recommend that your parents test out areas before buying. This is the one time that it is worth renting in an area before buying. Older Americans should follow all the rules we discussed in the chapter on location analysis, but as a final test they should get the area into their blood by living there for a brief period of time. For the same reason, older Americans buying their last house should negotiate a mortgage that has no prepayment penalties, enabling them to get out easily if they find they have made a mistake.

Financially, older Americans may be in a slightly different position than their children, but most of the rules of affordability are the same. While income may be reduced, older Americans will have the profits from the sale of their last home to count on. Still, I believe that older Americans should avoid putting a large down payment down on their retirement home, and certainly should avoid paying cash for their final home.

Leverage is a great gift bestowed on all of us by the capitalist system. There is no reason why that gift should only be available to young people. As I mentioned in an earlier chapter, at age eighty my parents took out a thirty-year mortgage on their retirement home. I believe that mortgages are, in fact, life extenders. And even if my parents don't live long enough to burn the mortgage (I wouldn't let them burn it anyway; they'd have to refinance), what's the difference? There is no shame in dying and leaving a mortgage. If the estate or a surviving co-owner wouldn't be able to pay monthly obligations, take out a term insurance policy which would pay down the mortgage to the level at which it could be afforded comfortably. Don't fall into the trap of buying the bank's mortgage life insurance. It isn't a worthwhile investment. For more information on this alternative to mortgage life insurance, see Appendix C.

All a bank should be concerned with is that the monthly payments are made. If a bank objects to giving older Americans long-term mortgages, they are guilty of discrimination just as surely as if they objected because of skin color or religion.

Affordability is figured exactly the same for older Americans as for first-time home buyers. Income from all sources, including social security, pensions and investment income should be taken into account. Here's where the proceeds from the sale of a home come in: They should take that hard-earned money and invest it in income-bearing instruments. In figuring out their monthly affordability, however, older Americans shouldn't stretch. They should be perfectly comfortable with the amount they can spend. Younger home buyers can count on having their incomes grow. Older Americans, unless they are investment wizards, should probably only count on keeping their income steady.

But this lack of "stretch" may be offset by the lower prices and higher values that are traditionally available in the retirement areas. By moving out of an urban center to a more rural area, home buyers can boost their buying power. Retirement areas often offer a host of other advantages to older buyers. Educational and recreational activities will be tailored to their interests. And adult communities often restrict the access of children and pets, creating a more relaxed, homogeneous environment.

This may also be the time for older buyers to think about moving from a single-family detached home—with all its upkeep expenses and problems—to attached housing: cooperative, condominium or association based.

Inspection is still an important part of the home-buying process for older Americans. In fact, if the retirement home is in a vacation area, inspection may be more important. Most vacation areas expose homes to a hard battering by the elements, be they desert winds or coastal storms. A professional inspection is therefore still a must.

Similarly, professional legal advice is essential for retirement home buyers as well as first-time buyers. Don't believe claims from brokers that the buying process in an established adult community is so boilerplate that attorneys aren't necessary. No matter how old the buyer is, the home purchase should always be a custom transaction. And make sure that the attorney used for the purchase is someone with experience in the area. Don't use a Wall Street attorney to buy a Fort Lauderdale condo. Your parents can keep their old accountant, but they should find a new lawyer.

By "buying down" to a smaller home, perhaps in a better, more suitable area, older Americans can take advantage of all the benefits of home ownership with fewer of the disadvantages. The ownership of a home is a lifelong process. Remember, we aren't looking to burn the mortgage. Today, if a home owner dies without a mortgage, he or she has probably made a mistake.

THE INS
AND OUTS
OF
MOVING

The part of buying a home most overlooked is the actual physical moving of your possessions from one place to another. In the excitement of buying a home, and the jubilation that follows, it's easy to forget that you'll have to move. This means that someone is going to have to transport your brass bed and grandma's old armoire from that apartment downtown to the farmhouse up in the country.

And that move can be not only an expensive proposition—generally costing at least $2,500—but a traumatic one as well. Fifty percent of consumers report some damage to their possessions while in transit. You can take a modicum of comfort in the fact that you aren't alone in this adventure. Approximately 20 percent of American families move every year, with the typical trip involving some three tons of cargo traveling over 1,000 miles. The moving industry is so large that federal and state government have seen fit to regulate transactions. All interstate moves (i.e., from one state to another) are made under rules established and enforced by the Interstate Commerce Commission, while intrastate moves (inside the same state) are governed by state regulatory agencies and departments.

Interstate moves are far and away more expensive and complicated. It's not unusual for a large move to cost the home owner over $4,000. The price is set according to a series of standard charges based on weight and distance. Added to that are charges for services such as packing and unpacking, appliance disconnection and boxes, if you need them. Packing costs three to five times more than unpacking, and boxes can cost anywhere from $1 to $10 each, depending on size. Heavy or bulky objects, such as rugs, carpets and pianos cost extra, and if they have to be moved up or down stairs, the added labor costs can be sizable. Since labor rates vary from one part of the country to another, it's best to check with local movers regarding fees for packing and unpacking.

Long distance moves are almost always made by the major van lines, which have agents representing them locally. Each truckload represents the possessions of more than one family. To determine the bills for individual customers, the driver will weigh the truck at a certified scale, then charge you for the difference in weight after your possessions have been loaded. Thanks to the ICC, you have the right to witness the weigh-in and even request a reweighing. You won't have to pay for the reweighing, but if the new total is higher, your bill will be increased.

Local moves are much more affordable. To move a small load of furniture, less than five hundred miles will probably cost less than $2,000. Short-distance move fees are based almost entirely on labor costs, figured at a set rate per hour. Locally owned and managed moving companies are the best for these short moves, rather than those with national reputations. Ask for recommendations from friends and relatives who have had a recent experience. Check with your state's agency that regulates moves for any information on the reputation and business record of all local and regional van lines. Another good place to check up on movers' credentials and reputations is the Better Business Bureau.

Regardless of whether your move is across town or across the country, get estimates. There are three types of estimates available: binding, nonbinding and a combination of the two. A *binding estimate* will involve a fee and will probably be higher, but will represent your final cost. There will be no surprises when the truck pulls up to your new home to unload. *Nonbinding estimates* are lower—intentionally, in order to draw in more business. You can expect that final costs will be 10 percent over the estimate. These estimates cost nothing, but may be worth just that. The *combination estimate* is not generally discussed by moving companies, but it represents your best deal. These "combo estimtates" bind the mover, not you. Your possessions are weighed on the day of the move and if they come in under the estimated poundage, you pay less than the quoted cost.

I recommend that you invite at least three companies in to offer estimates on your move. Present them with their precise responsibilities—the objects to be moved, the distance, the time involved, the services required—and make sure that each mover bids on exactly the same specifications. Prepare a checklist and present it to each company representative. This standardization of the estimate process will at least allow you to compare the same services, rather than the special package deal that companies provide to differentiate them from their competitors.

Make sure that any moving agreement you sign (generally called *bill of lading*) states specific dates for pickup and delivery. Moving companies hate to pin themselves down to a set day, and will request a string of three consecutive days on each end. If punctuality is essential, companies will guarantee pickup and delivery days, but will assess an added fee. Don't schedule moving days that are too close to your final day in your old home, or your first day of ownership of the new home. Weather, mechanical and traffic conditions can play havoc with schedules that are too tight. If you are unable to accept delivery, the mover will place your possessions in storage and charge a warehouse fee based on how much space your goods occupy.

Interstate movers must provide you with a copy of an ICC pamphlet entitled "Your Rights and Responsibilities When You Move," in addition to a copy of the company's performance record for the past year. Make sure your mover presents you with both.

Before agreeing to any moving agreement, check your home owner's insurance to see what coverage you have for damage that occurs during a move. Policies vary in their coverage of damage and loss during moves, and it is possible that you can add a temporary rider to your current policy to cover the move.

The moving companies themselves will offer insurance coverage—limited liability, added valuation or full value coverage—on items which they themselves pack. Limited liability often comes free with the moving charges, but only affords you sixty cents per pound. If that one pound antique jade figurine gets smashed, the mover will only pay sixty cents, even though it may be worth $600. Added valuation allows you to collect the replacement cost of damaged or lost goods, after depreciation has been figured in. It generally costs fifty cents for every $100 of the total value you attach to your load of possessions. There is a limit though, to the amount you can collect under an added valuation policy. The maximum is 125 percent of the number of pounds being shipped. In other words, if your total shipment weighed

5,000 pounds, the most you could collect on the damage or loss of items would be $7,500. Full value protection affords just that—full replacement cost with no deduction for depreciation. Each company's full value protection plan is different, with varying levels of deductibles. An average policy with no deductible costs approximately seventy-five cents per $100 of declared value; a $250 deductible policy costs thirty cents per $100; a $500 deductible policy is fifteen cents per $100; and a $1,000 deductible policy costs five cents per $100. Intrastate move liability is generally covered by local regulation, so check with the local mover or agent for details.

Once you have arranged for a mover, settled on a date and taken care of your insurance coverage, it's time to complete your personal paperwork in preparation for the move. Try to leave yourself six weeks to prepare. Begin by contacting your local school district and having your childrens' records transferred to the new district. Go to the post office and get change-of-address cards and send them to magazines, credit card companies and any other organizations that regularly send you mail. At the same time, fill out a forwarding request at the post office so that other mail will follow you to your new home. Call the phone and utility companies and set a date to have service disconnected in your old home and connected in your new home. If you are moving intrastate, try to have your new service connected that same day. Call the department of motor vehicles and have automobile records— license, registration and insurance card—updated to reflect your new address. Go to your banks and have accounts transferred to other branches of the same bank, or to a new bank. Notify all creditors that you are moving, and provide them with your new address. Cancel the newspaper and arrange for delivery at your new home. Talk to your doctor and dentist and have them transfer records if you are moving outside the area. Defrost and dry out refrigerators and freezers in preparation for the move. Arrange for cash and travelers checks for the trip to the new home, and to pay the mover. Pack small, valuable objects and important papers yourself, and bring them with you and your family. If the mover is going to pack for you, weed out your possessions prior to packing day. By law, movers are not allowed to throw anything out. If you don't empty the ashtray or take out the garbage, the movers will pack them up and deliver them to your new home.

As the mover loads boxes and furniture onto his truck, he will draw up an inventory list describing each item and its condition. Make sure that you understand any notations that are made on the inventory—it's your only proof that the jade figurine wasn't broken when it was loaded on the truck. If you don't agree with the mover's assessment of the condition of an item, note your objection on the inventory list. Don't sign the list until you have read it carefully and made any necessary corrections.

The mover will pull up to your new home and ask for payment before he unloads anything. Most moving companies accept cash, money orders, travelers checks and cashier's checks. None accept personal checks. Some of the major van lines are beginning to accept major credit cards. Agree on a method of payment before signing the agreement. If you have any particularly valuable possessions, consider tipping the movers before loading or unloading. Afterward, it could be too late.

Once the possessions arrive at your new home, check for obvious damage to furniture or to cartons and boxes. Don't unpack and inspect every item looking for hidden damage. Instead, look for obvious problems. If you discover any problems once you have unpacked, leave the damaged item in the packaging so that an agent from the company can examine it. Claim forms are available from either the moving company's agent or the home office. Claims must be filed within nine months of the move.

With a little preparation and planning, a move—even across the country—can be relatively painless. And, as long as you have adequately prepared your insurance coverage, you'll find that a move, while complicated and disorienting, can be risk free.

INSURANCE
IN THE
HOME-
BUYING
PROCESS

While it is always important to have adequate insurance, you must pay special attention to your coverage and risk protection during the home-acquisition process. The stakes have never been higher. Now you will be responsible, by agreement, for the adequate protection of a third party—your mortgagee—in addition to yourself and your family.

The principal of insurance with which you will be concerning yourself is a *homeowner's insurance policy,* which covers the replacement value of the home and (optimistically) your belongings inside the home. It may also include any number of variations, including public liability insurance—in case someone is injured on your property.

Your mortgagee will require that you have a comprehensive policy on the dwelling, with enough coverage at least to protect his cash investment. In fact, your insurance policy will list the mortgagee along with you as a beneficiary. Don't worry about the lender's insurance demands. The insurance requirements spelled out in the mortgage will be less than those you will actually need.

Homeowner's insurance for a condominium is slightly different. One major policy will cover the entire complex. You pay a prorated share of the premium as part of your monthly maintenance fee. Once again, the mortgagee will be a beneficiary of this policy. In addition, you will need your own policy, covering your particular unit and its contents.

The insurance coverage needs of cooperative owners are identical to those in a tenant's policy, covering solely the contents of the individual unit. The co-op corporation has its own master policy which insures the structure itself.

At least once during the title closing, the bank's representative might ask you if you would like to take out *mortgage life insurance.* He'll offer you a policy that covers the unpaid portion of the mortgage and seems to have a very reasonable premium. Don't fall for it. It's exceptionally profitable for the bank and a waste of money for you. You would be able to get better coverage for less money by taking out a "reducing term" life insurance policy in the amount of the mortgage.

I'm not a believer in mortgage insurance, unless the death of a co-owner would actually reduce the ability of the survivor to make monthly mortgage payments. In that case, I advise that you take out a term policy that would pay down the mortgage by the amount of the principal attributable to the lost monthly income. In other words, if the deceased contributed $100 a month to the mortgage payment, then the contribution would amount to $10,000 of the principal (based on a thirty-year term at 10 percent interest). Go to a mortgage table and see how much principal is represented by the potential income loss, then insure to cover only that amount.

Title insurance is a one-time expense that protects the mortgagee and, optionally, the borrower against unclear title to the property you are buying. Most lenders will require that you pay for their title insurance. For an additional small premium, the title company will protect you as well. It's worthwhile, just in case that one-in-a-million title problem involves your property. The fees for title insurance are often regulated. If they aren't in your state, have your lawyer shop around assiduously, since the premiums are set capriciously.

Private mortgage insurance is available from a series of providers who will, for a sizable premium, guarantee to the bank that your debt to them will be paid if you fall into default. It is most often used when you are asking the bank to exceed its normal loan-to-value ratio and put up 90 percent or more of the purchase price. The annual premiums for this kind of policy could amount to as much as 1 percent of the loan's principal. Luckily, you would keep such a policy in force only for the period of time that the loan-to-value ratio is above the bank's norm—usually no more than three-to-five years.

If your home is in a fragile environmental area, threatened by unusually hazardous weather conditions, such as flooding or earthquakes, there are special types of insurance available. The federal government has established the National Flood Insurance program to protect coastal areas (that are subject to severe conditions) from flooding, storms or hurricanes. In addition, twenty-six states belong to the Fair Access to Insurance Requirements Plan (FAIR), which offers insurance to those who have difficulty getting protection for a high risk property.

Whatever the extent of your insurance needs, pending ownership of a home requires that you reexamine your current policies and search for the best policies available. The independent insurance broker you selected in Chapter Eight can be an invaluable aid in this effort.

SHOPPING FOR A MORTGAGE: YOUR CHECKLIST

The following checklist may be used for your comparison shopping interview with each bank for whatever type of home or mortage you need.

Use one sheet for each bank to create a compendium of its various loan plan offerings.

Lending institution_____

Telephone_____

Contact_____

Bank address (to be used for application submission)

_____

_____

_____

FOR ADJUSTABLE RATE LOANS

Ask the following questions:

	Plan A	Plan B	Plan C
1. Interest Rate			
2. Adjustment period			
3. Index			
4. Adjustment period cap			
5. Lifetime cap			
6. Convertible? If so, when and cost:			

7. Loan term			
8. Points			
9. Origination fee			
10. Loan-to-value ratio (LTV)			
11. APR (Average Percentage Rate)			

FOR FIXED RATE LOANS

Ask the following questions:

1. Interest rate			
2. Points			
3. Origination fee			
4. Loan term			
5. Loan-to-value ratio (LTV)			
6. APR (Average Percentage Rate			

FOR ALL LOANS

Ask the following questions:

Is non-income verification
available? (yes or no)

Is "stretch" (nonstandard
LTV) available?

Debt-to-income
ratio

Application fee

Appraisal fee

Credit check fee

Credit reporting
bureau used

Closing attorney
fee (bank)

Prepayment
penalty
(yes or no)
if yes, amount and when

Bank's response and
processing time
for commitment
and closing

Length of
commitment
(30, 60, 90 days, etc.)

Renewable,
(yes or no)
if yes: same rate?
           new rate?
           procedure?

Rate lock-in
if yes: at application?
           at commitment?
           at closing?
           extra cost?

Special programs
available

Preferred customer
benefits

Other comments:

DOCUMENTATION REQUIRED WITH APPLICATION: CHECKLIST

Fees

Paystub

Tax returns

Profit & Loss statement
(for self-employed)

Contact of sale

Offering plan
(for cooperatives and condos)
including: proprietary lease
by-laws

_____

Building financials
(for cooperatives and more
than two-family dwellings)

_____

Other:

_____

_____

_____

REGIONAL TRENDS

Here's a look at some major metropolitan areas and the prevailing conditions in each market.

THE NORTHEAST CORRIDOR

The home-buyer's market in the Northeast has lost some steam since the stock market tremor of October 1987. Demand has abated as potential buyers waited to see if more shock waves were on the way. Private sellers have refused to give in to the temporary slump and are holding fast to their prices. Developers, on the other hand, faced with a glut of units, have been making price concessions. This region, once a strong seller's market, is slowly shifting to a buyer's market.

BOSTON The newly built home market in Boston, while still warm, is leveling off a bit. Single-family homes being built, will be up over the average for the past few years. Prices on these new dwellings are also stabilizing, after almost 20 percent rises in the past couple of years. $450,000 seems to be the top price, with homes under $250,000 drawing a great deal of attention. Homes under that price are getting increasingly difficult to find. New multi-family dwellings in Boston, mostly condominiums, are slowing down even more than homes. A glut on the market, caused by a drop in the number of speculative investors, is driving down prices and slowing construction. The popular range seems to be $125,000 to $175,000. The existing Boston home market is shifting to a buyer's market, with prices dropping—but only slightly. No increase is expected over the next 12 to 18 months.

HARTFORD New construction of both single-family and multi-family dwellings is slowing down in Hartford, and prices are remaining stable or increasing. Like most of the Northeast, the market in Hartford is expensive (though still not as high as Fairfield County). The hot price range at the moment seems to be $150,000 to $225,000, while new condos run approximately $110,000. The top end of the single-family home market appears to be close to $350,000. Townhouses, which represent a large portion of the Hartford market, are getting harder to find and afford, since so many offices are relocating to Hartford and more and more jobs are being created. Existing homes under $100,000 are scarce. There is a decided lack of moderately priced housing, though there is talk of construction along the long-neglected waterfront.

NEW YORK/LONG ISLAND/NORTH-CENTRAL NEW JERSEY New construction in the New York/Long Island area is dipping for single-family homes, and slightly down for multi-family dwellings. In the past two years, owners have enjoyed appreciation as high as 30 percent. In North-central New Jersey, new construction remains at the same level as in past years mostly because of the moratorium on building. Resale homes can be found for $160,000, while new homes are well over $200,000. A glut of condos has hit the market in Manhattan, but resales and prewar co-ops, while still in demand, have leveled off in price and are going at the low end for about $100,000 for a studio or one bedroom to over a million for a luxury, family-sized unit. It is still the most expensive market in the nation, with median home prices averaging $200,000. But since the October 1987 crash, which hit the New York economy harder than most areas, the market has been softening, giving buyers more choice and negotiating power than in recent years. The outer boroughs are witnessing a rising tide of renovations and conversions. Suburban demand has slowed down somewhat, but it's still a seller's market.

PHILADELPHIA New construction in Philadelphia is still rising, particularly in single-family homes. Sales are still up, and virtually no new homes are available for under $100,000. Even inexpensive communities have risen above the $100,000 mark. Prices on homes range from $200,000 in Montgomery, $125,000 in Chester, $150,000 in Bucks, to over $300,000 for subdivided estates on the Main Line. The rapidly rising prices over the past years in the hot Main Line area are expected to stabilize.

BALTIMORE With clear evidence of overbuilding downtown and in the surrounding areas, the new construction market has slowed down, both in multi- and single-family dwellings. Single-family homes in Baltimore and Howard counties are going for $200,000. Townhouses, which make up almost half the market in this city, are going for prices from $90,000 to $190,000. Demand is increasing, as are prices—which have been called outrageous for Baltimore.

WASHINGTON, D.C. The boom in Washington, D.C. housing seems to have abated. Buyers are discouraged by increased prices and long commutes into the center city area, though highway improvements have reportedly begun. New single-family home construction continues to increase, while multi-family dwelling construction has slowed dramatically. Single-family homes and townhouses within an hour's drive of D.C. can't be found for $160,000 or $100,000, respectively. Single-family homes are generally running for $180,000. Many of the suburban areas that were denigrated in the past are now seeing a resurgence of interest.

THE MIDWEST

CHICAGO New single-family home construction is rising in Chicago, while multi-family home construction is the healthiest in the nation. Prices are rising approximately 8 percent annually in the most popular areas, with many now above $150,000. The Naperville area is most competitive, with new single-family and multi-family homes averaging $136,000, though there are still some units available at lower prices. Lower-priced, single-family home development is moving to the north and west of the city. Arlington Heights homes are ranging from $160,000 to $210,000. In the western suburbs, a complete range of single-family homes—including townhouses, old and new homes and estates—is available. But in the city, single-family homes are in demand and selling at rapidly increasing prices.

CINCINNATI New home construction in Cincinnati is primarily single-family homes. Demand in the area seems extremely high, with single-family homes in the $150,000 to $300,000 price range moving best. Townhouses and condominiums cost approximately $60,000 to $150,000 and $35,000 to $70,000 respectively. With a combined population of over 200,000, Kentucky, Clermont and Warren counties across the Ohio River are becoming increasingly popular because of the new improved beltline, providing quick access to the metropolitan area.

DETROIT New single-family home construction is up in Detroit, while multi-family home construction is down. Prices are rising rapidly, especially for single-family homes, since demand is very high at this time. Blue-collar communities are doing well, with homes in the $90,000 to $120,000 price range. Condos range from $90,000 to $180,000. Existing homes are in extremely high demand in this crowded city.

KANSAS CITY New single-family home construction remains steady in the Kansas City market. Building activity in the multi-family units is highest since 1982. In Johnson County, which is leading the state in apartment construction, homes are running from $100,000 to $150,000. With a glut of luxury condos, apartment sales are slow, but steady absorption is apparent since more people are moving into downtown. Entry-level homes in Jackson County are priced from $70,000 to $90,000.

MINNEAPOLIS/ST. PAUL In the Twin Cities area, single-family homes are being built—and selling—in large numbers, while multi-family homes are being built less often and are dropping in price. Single-family homes in the Eagan area, Plymouth, Eden Prairie and Burnsville are selling in the $75,000 to $120,000 range. Many condominiums that were priced from $80,000 to $300,000 are remaining on the market.

ST LOUIS The situation in St. Louis echoes that of the Twin Cities, with single-family homes selling well and multi-family homes slowing down. The fastest-growing price range is from $120,000 to $150,000. Prime condominiums in central locations are still selling for over $350,000.

THE SOUTH

ATLANTA Even though new single-family home construction is dropping rapidly, Atlanta remains the scene of much new building. Single-family homes ranging from $80,000 to $110,000 are selling rapidly, while higher-priced homes are staying on the market longer. Prices continue to increase, and lenders seem a bit hesitant. Cluster homes in the vicinity of downtown are selling at the same price as single-family homes farther out in the suburbs. Gwinett, East Cobb and the Fulton-Roswell-Alpharetta areas are selling well in the $120,000 to $160,000 range. Entry-level homes are priced in the $55,000 to $70,000 range and those located south of the Atlanta airport are also selling well. The townhouse market has slowed down dramatically, with units in the $175,000 to $180,000 range staying on the market for a long time.

AUSTIN The Austin market is a classic example of a buyer's market, with new home construction way down, and units being discounted from 5 to 25 percent, depending on the original price. One developer is rumored to be offering a free Yugo with each unit sold.

DALLAS/FORT WORTH Another buyer's market, with new construction down. Closings were up, at prices that made no money for developers. Pricing remains flat, or even decreasing. Homes in this region are staying on the market an average of six months. Condominiums are being converted to rentals, since sales are few and far between.

HOUSTON New construction has slowed to a crawl in Houston. The newer homes however, are selling more rapidly than existing ones. The homes selling best are in the $100,000 to $125,000 range. While some units are selling at $80,000, none are going quickly. In this desperately unstable economy, at the moment there are good buys to be found from oil farmers looking to recoup. There may be a change on the horizon, however, since employment growth seems inevitable after a loss of over 30,000 jobs in 1986.

MIAMI/FORT LAUDERDALE In Miami, condos are beginning to sell—again. There is still a large oversupply of luxury units, putting a lot of pressure on the single-family market, but they are selling steadily at decreased prices averaging $71,000, as compared to 1986 when the average was $86,000—though there are still beachfront condos going for

$450,000 and up. Single-family homes are being built rapidly throughout the area, with sales strongest in Kendall. Prices in Dade and Broward counties range from $70,000 to $120,000. It has been said that the action is moving north towards Palm Beach, but renovated Deco on South Beach may just make it, since some new developers seem determined to stick it out.

NASHVILLE This Tennessee city is a strong seller's market for single-family homes with units selling in the $80,000 to $100,000 range. Some are up to $150,000, moving in the better areas. There is a boom in apartment construction, and it looks like buyers are buying, especially near the airport corridor's new facilities.

NORTHFOLK / VIRGINIA BEACH / NEWPORT NEWS This Virginia region may be in the midst of a change from a seller's to a buyer's market. Single-family home building is up, but condominium building and sales are down. The seller's market was created by increased immigration in past years, which has slowed noticeably. Fast-selling single-family homes are in the $60,000–$90,000 range in areas such as Newport News, Hampton, Chesapeake and Virginia Beach.

ORLANDO The Orlando market is moving towards a buyer's market. Multi-family building has screeched to a halt, and the available units don't seem to be moving. Those selling best have excellent amenities, and are priced between $60,000 and $95,000. However, very few single-family homes are available, with those under $90,000 selling best. Higher-priced homes are being offered at a discount.

RALEIGH-DURHAM This area is a victim of over-building—a definite buyer's market with single-family homes and condos staying on the market for quite some time. Single-family homes in under $90,000 are selling best. A resurgence in corporations moving to the area may shift the tide back to a seller's market.

SAN ANTONIO The Alamo city is a strong buyer's market. Homes in the $60,000 to $90,000 range were the most in demand, though they are few and far between. Higher-priced homes are moving slowly, and condominiums are being discounted. Auctions are being used in the community, but are said to have had little impact.

TAMPA/ST. PETERSBURG This Gulf Coast region is a combination of seller's and buyer's markets, depending on the area of the cities. Northeast Hillsborough is hot, while Lutz is relatively inactive. Brandon homes in the $80,000 to $100,000 range are moving well. Northwest Hillsborough sales have slowed, while Carrollwood Village and coastal Pasco County remain stable.

THE WEST

DENVER A buyer's market for the next few years, with single-family homes level and condominiums dropping in price. The most competitive part of the market is in the $125,000 to $225,000 single-family home. Condominiums are being auctioned at 30 to 50 percent under list price. An attempt to lure new business and employment should help. There are plenty of buyers for homes under $100,000, but higher-priced units up to $500,000 are reduced a number of times over several months before selling.

LAS VEGAS A seller's market, with single-family homes in the $60,000 to $80,000 range moving rapidly. Condominiums, many on golf courses, are coming on to the market. Competition has increased in single-family homes in the $125,000 to $150,000 range.

LOS ANGELES / ORANGE COUNTY / RIVERSIDE/SAN BERNARDINO Seller's market with increased single-family home sales brought on by increased employment. Market competition centered on homes over $175,000. Condominiums and townhouses very competitive, with prices ranging $115,000 in Santa Margarita to $220,000 in Irving. Resale listings are few and far beween, with demand very high.

PHOENIX A buyer's market with homes in the $70,000 to $100,000 range being most competitive. Building continues to accommodate the increase in business and employment. In the southeast area, single-family homes are selling quickly at $120,000 to $140,000. Scottsdale condominiums in the $150,000 to $200,000 range are staying on the market for long periods of time. Units are also selling in the Tempe and Mesa areas, since the new freeway systems are making commutes bearable.

SACRAMENTO A seller's market in both single- and multi-family homes. The most competitive price market is the single-family home for $85,000 to $135,000. Lower-priced units are also available, but the demand is high. The area with a huge amount of available land, is one of the only places in the country experiencing such rampant new construction because of the strong base of government spending there.

SAN DIEGO San Diego looks like an extremely hot seller's market, with single-family homes under $100,000 selling rapidly, and moving off the market quickly in other price ranges as well. Planned communities and golf course developments from $100,000 to $200,000 are very much in demand.

SAN FRANCISCO/OAKLAND/SAN JOSE Another hot sellers market, with both single-family and multi-family homes under $300,000 moving quickly off the market. Hottest homes are single-family units under $200,000 in West Contra Costa or Vallejo-Bencia. Condos, which were languishing on the market, are becoming more in demand. Single-family homes in Redwood City priced at $600,000 are selling rapidly. New homes being built to the east and north of the city priced at approximately $140,000 are expected to be hot.

SEATTLE A surging seller's market, with single-family homes in the $90,000 to $120,000 range moving off the market quickly. Lake Washington and Snohomish County areas are extremely competitive. Prices are rising 10 percent. Condos, on the other hand, are available in these areas. Average prices are around $60,000. Construction has definitely slowed since

1986, since more people are buying single-family units for almost comparable prices.

It's difficult to predict future trends in the real estate market. Construction is generally planned three to four years in advance, and always seems too early or too late to catch onto buying trends. Because of this, real estate usually lags behind the rest of the economic indicators, and suffers plateaus that often have little or nothing to do with the rest of the economy. With that said, there are certain truths that will remain constant: People will always want homes—perhaps in new configurations or in new areas—and there will always be anxiety and stress in the purchase. The best way to avoid this stress is to dispell those unwarranted fears and to set realistic goals for the transaction.

GLOSSARY

Abstract of title. A summary of a property's history, listing all changes in ownership, liens, mortgages, charges or any other actions that may affect the property's title.

Acceleration clause. One of the standard sections of a mortgage which allows the lender to demand full payment of a loan if the borrower does not make a scheduled payment on time.

Access. The way an owner gets to and from a property, for example, a driveway, a street, a path and so on.

Accountability. Ultimate responsibility for a property or money or for controlling the documents which concern property or money.

Acre. A measure of land equaling 43,560 square feet. A "builder's acre" is 200 × 200 feet or 40,000 square feet.

Addendum, or *rider.* Something added, as to a contract. On a contract, an addendum is usually on a separate page and attached to the standard contract. It should be signed separately.

Adjustable-rate mortgage. A type of loan in which the interest rate may be changed periodically to reflect market conditions.

Agency. A fiduciary relationship in which one party acts on behalf of another in a real estate transaction, negotiating the sale, purchase, leasing or exchanging of property.

Agent.   A person who represents another with the latter's approval.

Air rights.   The rights of an owner to use a specified amount of space above a property. The right extends to the responsibility for light, noise, pollution and any other infringements. A famous example is the Pan Am Building above Grand Central Station.

ALTA Title Insurance Policy.   A type of broad coverage insurance designed to protect against any kind of title defect. Specific risks, such as survey matters, unrecorded mechanic liens, water and mineral rights and rights of parties in possession are automatically covered.

Amenities.   Extra attractions or features on or affecting a piece of property such as a health club, doorman, view of the river and so on.

Amortization.   The system of repaying a loan over a specified period of time.

Annual Percentage Rate (APR).   The actual yearly cost of credit in percentage terms.

Apportionment, or *adjustments.*   Expenses such as maintenance, taxes, fees and so on, that are prorated and divided between seller and buyer, especially if the closing is held at some time other than the first of the month or the end of a tax period.

Appreciation.   The amount by which a property increases in value.

Appraisal, or *valuation.*   The opinion of an expert on the value of property, or some interest therein. This is usually accompanied by an appraisal report, showing the estimated value and any reservations or qualifications attached to it.

Appurtenances.   Things which have been added to or are used integrally with a property and therefore pass on to the buyer, such as a gate, driveway or garden.

Assessed valuation. An appraisal of property by a municipal official for the purpose of taxation. The trend in America is toward 100 percent valuation.

Balloon payment. The unamortized principal of a mortgage or any type of loan, which is to be paid in one lump sum.

Bank check. An obligation by the issuing bank which guarantees payment of a check.

Binder. One of the first steps in the buying process. A written agreement accompanied by a check to acknowledge that the buyer and seller both intend to carry through the transaction; an earnest money receipt.

Binding. Enforceable and legal, as in a contract.

Bona fide. In good faith; to be trusted; free from deception.

Broker. See *Real estate broker.*

Builder's warranty. A written assurance from a builder that all work done conforms with previously set standards, such as the architect's plan and specifications.

Building codes. Regulations issued by local or state agencies that govern alterations, design, quality and construction details of a residence.

Buyer's market. The condition that exists when the supply of property strongly exceeds the demand, so that buyers are able to bargain more effectively, with more choices available.

Cancellation clause. The section of a contract that gives the buyer or seller the right to get out of a contract if some stated condition or situation occurs, such as failure to obtain mortgage financing. Also, see *Contingency.*

Capital appreciation. The increase in a property's value beyond what was paid for it.

Caveat emptor. "Let the buyer beware." The purchaser examines and purchases property at his/her own risk.

Certificate of occupancy (CO, or *C of O).* An official document stating that premises, having passed all required inspections, are constructed in accordance with building codes and are fit for public or private use.

Certified check. A check that is as good as cash since, the bank that issues it guarantees that the funds are available. Certified checks are generally required at the closing for the payment of the balance of the purchase price, some bank and title charges, attorney fees and other such fees.

Cloud. See *Title, cloud on.*

Closing. The final step in a real estate transaction. This is when title and other documentation are transferred and money changes hands. Variously describes the mutual signing of the contract or the bank's disbursement of mortgage proceeds. Also, see *Settlement.*

Closing costs. Those costs that are required at the closing, in addition to the actual purchase price of the property. These typically include adjustments, bank fees, attorney fees, brokerage and title company fees and so on.

Closing statement, or *closing account.* A summary and reconcilation of all expenses, adjustments and disbursements involved during any closing.

Collateral. Something of value that is used as security to ensure that a loan will be repaid.

Common law. The type of law that is based on custom (English law) rather than on codified law (Roman law).

Condominium. A type of housing unit in which the owners own their apartment, plus an undivided portion of the common area.

Consideration. A sum of money, or anything of value that must accompany a contract in order for it to be binding.

Contingency. A provision within a contract that keeps it from becoming binding until certain conditions are satisfied.

Contract. A legally binding, enforceable agreement between two parties to do some specified thing. To be valid, a real estate contract must be in writing; must be signed and dated by all parties involved; and includes the consideration, a description of the property, the designated date and place for delivery of the deed and all other material terms agreed upon by the parties involved.

Convey. To transfer real property from one person to another.

Conveyance. Any document, except a will, by which a title is transferred.

Cooperative, or *co-op.* A type of housing or ownership where buyers purchase shares in the corporation that owns the building, rather than purchase the physical apartment. A proprietary lease accompanies such a purchase allowing the owner to live in the premises. This kind of ownership is really ownership of personal property rather than real estate.

Deed. A document legally transferring a real-estate title.

Default. Failure to comply with the terms of an agreement, especially repeated nonpayment of a scheduled mortgage payment.

Demographic. Relating to population study and characteristics.

Demography. The study of population characteristics, trends and patterns.

Density. The number of living spaces, commercial units and/or the number of people per acre or other measure of land.

Depreciation. Gradual decrease in the market value of property, especially because of age, physical deterioration, obsolescence or economic conditions. Also, for bookkeeping purposes and income tax purposes, a deduction from gross income to provide for the recapture of investment in a wasting asset other than land.

Down payment. The initial amount of cash you advance towards your investment, usually a percentage of the purchase price.

Easement. The limited right of one person to use another's property, often for a specific purpose.

Economic base. The economic activity of an area or community that exports goods or services in return for money or income. Often this is the activity for which a community is famous (though not necessarily successful), as oil in Texas.

Eminent domain. The right of a government to take private property for public use without the owner's consent as long as they pay the owner a reasonable fee for compensation.

Encroachment. A building or section of a structure that intrudes upon someone else's property.

Encumbrance. A restriction that has been imposed on a property's title, often affecting its value. Common encumbrances are liens, liabilities, outstanding mortgage loans, unpaid taxes and so on.

Equity. The value an owner has on a property excluding the unpaid mortgage balance or any other claims.

Equity buildup. The increase in the owner's financial interest because of mortgage loan amortization and/or appreciation in the total value of the land.

Escheat. Reversion of property to the state because there are no heirs available and the owner did not make a will granting the property to anyone else.

Escrow. Money or documents which are held by a neutral third party until certain conditions of an agreement are met.

Escrow account. The bank account into which escrow funds are deposited and from which they are disbursed. Escrow monies may also be deposited in a certificate of deposit or other interest-bearing security.

Execute. To make legally binding, usually by signing.

Federal National Mortgage Association, Fannie Mae (FNMA). A government-sponsored, privately owned corporation that supplements private mortgage operations by buying and selling FHA, VA and conventional loans.

Federal Housing Authority (FHA). An agency created within HUD (defined below) to insure mortgages on residential property, requiring a relatively low down payment.

Fee, fee simple, fee simple absolute. The most absolute type of private ownership of an interest in real estate that includes all rights of possession, control, use and disposition, even by inheritance. The only limitations on such ownership are police power, taxation, eminent domain and escheat.

Fiduciary. A person who acts in a position of trust or confidence, and who is legally accountable.

Fixtures. Items included in a real estate sale that are attached to the property in such a fashion that their removal would create damage. Examples are sink, lighting fixtures, storm windows and so on.

Foreclosure. Legal proceedings begun by a lender to deny a borrower his or her ownership and possession privileges and legally request a sale in order to obtain repayment on a defaulted debt.

Federal Home Loan Mortgage Corporation, Freddie Mac (FHLMC.) A secondary mortgage market affiliated with the Federal Home Loan Bank System, authorized to buy and sell conventional, FHA and VA loans.

Garden apartment. An apartment unit in a smaller apartment house (multiunit residences) with land.

Gentrification. The process of displacing low- to moderate-income families and replacing them with higher-income tenants in order to "upgrade" a neighborhood.

Government-assisted housing. Lower-priced housing units that are subsidized by local, state or federal governments.

Government National Mortgage Association, Ginnie Mae (GNMA). A federal government corporation designed to handle special assistance functions for certain FHA and VA loans, and to guarantee certain securities backed by mortgage loans.

Grace period. A length of time within which to fulfill a commitment or obligation after the original deadline has not been met.

Grantee. The person or party to whom real estate is conveyed; the buyer.

Grantor. The person or party conveying an interest in realty, as in a deed signed by a seller.

Housing code. A set of municipal standards which must be met by all housing units to guarantee that dwellings are safe for human habitation.

United States Department of Housing and Urban Development (HUD). The governmental agency from which almost all federally funded housing programs flow.

Improved land. Land prepared for development by sewers, water, roads and the like, and on which buildings have been erected.

Installment payment. The process of paying off a mortgage or other loan in periodic payments, usually monthly.

Installment sales contract, or *"land contract."* A contract which makes provisions for the buyer to occupy or use property but not receive the title until certain payments or obligations are made.

Instrument. Any written legal document.

Interest. A rent or charge for borrowing money; the quality of ownership.

Joint tenancy. Ownership whereby two or more people have an undividable share of property, so that if one owner dies, the others automatically retain possession, receiving the interest of the deceased.

Judgment. A court decree to state officially that a person owes someone else a specified amount of money.

Land. The solid ground. Often used interchangeably with realty.

Land bank. The accumulation of vacant land for an unannounced or undetermined use.

Land contract. See *Installment sales contract.*

Land, raw. Land that can be built on, but does not have any preparation or improvements such as pipes, electricity, water or roads.

Lease. A contract allowing a person possession of real estate in exchange for payment, usually monthly rental, to the owner of the property.

Legal description. A specific and unique identification of a parcel of real estate that is recognized and acknowledged by law.

Leverage. The use of borrowed money combined with the lowest amount possible of one's own money to buy property. This practice often allows for a higher rate of return on an investment. An economic analogy to the physical use of a lever to gain a mechanical advantage.

Lien. An enforceable claim on property because the owner has an outstanding debt.

Liability. A disadvantage or drawback; a legal responsibility and obligation to another.

Liquidity. The speed at which an investment can be converted to cash.

Listing. An agreement to employ a real estate agent to represent and sell a piece of property or the actual property that is for sale.

Loan-to-value ratio. The percentage that a property is financed by a mortgage loan.

Location analysis. The identification and study of environment, situs, linkages, accessibility and other external factors as they relate to the use, utility and value of a site or property.

Market, primary mortgage. A market made up of lenders who supply mortgage funds directly to borrowers, such as savings and loan associations and banks.

Market, secondary mortgage. A market in mortgages made up of mortgage bankers and brokers who originate loans, and lenders, such as insurance companies and mutual savings banks, who place or invest funds.

Market value. Believed to be the most probable selling price for a price of property or the highest price that a ready, willing and able buyer will pay, and the lowest price of a ready, willing and able seller will accept for a piece of property.

Marketable title. A title that is clear of any clouds or encumbrances.

Maturity date. The predetermined date at which a mortgage or other financial obligation must be paid in its entirety.

Metes and bounds. A legal description of a property which is defined by directions and distances.

Mortgage. The legal document that provides real property as security for the repayment of a debt or obligation.

Mortgagee. The person or institution that lends money.

Mortgagor. The person or party that borrows money, using the purchased property, or some other property, as security for the loan.

Mortgage company, or *mortgage broker.* A financial go-between that offers mortgages to buyers and then sells them to another investor for a profit.

Multiple listing. An agreement among various real estate brokers to share information on available property so that it can receive as much publicity as possible. Commissions are split between the selling and listing brokers.

Offer. A written or verbal proposal to buy property at a specified price.

Offering plan, or *prospectus.* A document, usually in bound form, that is put together by the condominium or cooperative sponsors to detail the specifics of an offer and the procedures of how the project will be run. It should contain a floor plan, location, prices and layouts of units, procedures to purchase and material conditions of ownership. Also see *Red herring.*

Option. The exclusive right to purchase or lease a property for a specified price.

Origination fee. A charge by the lender for granting the mortgage.

Planned Unit Development (PUD). A residential complex in which different types of housing are clustered together in ways that are not traditionally allowed under most zoning laws, in order to provide open common spaces and topo-graphically harmonious landscape.

Points, or *discount.*   A fee that a lender charges for granting the mortgage. One point is equal to 1 percent of the total value of the loan.

Power of attorney.   A written document that grants one person the legal right to act as an agent for another in signing papers, deeds, titles and so on.

Premises.   The land in question and everything attached to it.

Prepayment.   The payment of a loan fully or partially before it is due.

Principal.   The amount of money that has been borrowed or the balance that is still owed.

Promissory note.   A statement signed by the debtor acknowledging a debt and the terms under which it is to be repaid.

Property.   The right or interest of an individual in lands or other goods to the exclusion of all others. Real property rights include possession, control, enjoyment and disposition.

Proprietary lease, or *occupancy agreement.*   The lease granting a tenant-shareholder in a cooperative the right to occupy an apartment.

Prorate.   To divide, distribute or assess proportionately.

Prospectus.   See *Offering plan.*

Real estate.   An asset, commodity or type of property, more accurately described as "realty," that begins with land and includes all permanent improvements to the land.

Real property   (as opposed to personal property). Land, buildings and anything permanently attached to them. See *Fixture.*

Real estate broker.   A person who has passed the state brokers test and represents others in real estate transactions.

Anyone running a real estate office is required to be a broker.

Real estate salesperson. A person who has passed a state examination for that position and is working under a broker.

Real estate taxes, or *property taxes.* Charges on land and buildings that are collected by local governing agencies as their primary source of revenue.

Realtor. A real estate broker who is a member of the National Association of Realtors, a professional organization.

Reconciliation. In appraising, the process of resolving differences in indications of market value to reach a final, conclusive estimate of value.

Recreation lease. A legal agreement allowing owners of certain condominiums to use the complex's pool, health club or other amenities.

Red herring. A preliminary offering plan which is used until the formal offering plan is approved by the appropriate agencies. Sponsors can show prospective co-op or condo buyers the "red herring", but cannot sell apartments or units without showing the formal prospectus. Also, see *Offering plan.*

Refinance. To pay off one loan by taking out another one on the same property.

Report of title. A document that is required before title insurance can be issued. It includes the name of the owner, a legal description of the property and the status of taxes, liens and anything else affecting the marketability of the title.

Real Estate Settlement Procedures Act (RESPA). A federal law applying to institutionally made first-mortgage loans to finance the purchase or ownership of one-family residences.

Restriction. Any type of limitation to control the use of a property.

Right of survivorship. The right granted to all parties in a joint ownership, stipulating that upon the death of one party the others receive full ownership. Right of survivorship is the basic difference between buying a property as joint tenants and tenants in common.

Seller's market. The condition that exists when the demand for property strongly exceeds the supply, so that sellers are able to bargain for and get higher prices.

Settlement. Final accounting and conclusion in a buy-sell or refinancing transaction. Also, see *Closing.*

Settlements costs. See *Closing costs.*

Shared appreciation mortgage (SAM). Arrangement whereby lender shares in any value increase in mortgage property.

Site analysis. The identification and study of characteristics, such as size and shape, topography and road improvements, that affect the value and marketability of a site.

Situs. Locational considerations in a piece of property, such as accessibility, exposure and personal preference.

Specific performance. A court order that compels a party to carry out the terms of an executed contract.

Sponsor. The individual or corporation that converts a rental complex into a cooperative or condominium.

Square foot. The measure of land or floor space used to describe the size of a property being sold. If a room measures 20 feet by 30 feet, the area is 600 square feet.

Statute of Frauds. Legislation that requires, among other things, that all contracts creating or transferring an interest in land or realty be in writing. The intent is to prevent perjured testimony and fraudulent proofs by disallowing oral testimony to interfere with or alter the terms of a written agreement.

Survey. The mapping process by which a parcel of land is measured and its area ascertained.

Tax avoidance. The governing of one's affairs, taking into consideration all aspects of the tax laws in order to pay the lowest amount of taxes legally permitted.

Tax base. The total assessed value of all property in a tax district.

Time is of the essence. A phrase used in a contract which makes failure to perform by a specified date a material breach or violation of the agreement.

Title. Ownership of property. For real estate, a lawful claim, supported by evidence of ownership.

Title, chain of. The succession of all previous owners, title holders of a specified property, going back to a reasonable starting point.

Title, cloud on. Anything that might affect the salability of a property, including a judgment, lien or mortgage, or claim against a right to use.

Title, marketable. A title that is readily salable to an interested, reasonable, prudent, intelligent buyer at market value.

Title company. A company organized to ensure title to real property.

Title insurance. Protection against financial loss due to defects in the title of real property that existed but were not known at the time of purchase of the insurance policy.

Title report. The results of a title search which should include the name of the owner, the legal description of a property, the status of the taxes, any other liens and encumbrances and sometimes the results of a property survey.

Trust-deed. An instrument used in lieu of a mortgage in certain areas of the country. In this type of loan, a third-party trustee (not the lender) holds the title to the property until the loan is paid off.

Underwriter. A mortgage analyst.

Usury. The illegal practice of lending money at a rate higher than is permitted by law.

Valuation. Estimated or determined value.

Veteran's Administration (VA). A federal government agency that aids veterans in obtaining housing, especially by guaranteeing loans with relatively low down payments.

Void. Canceled, not legally binding.

Waiver. The renunciation or surrender of some claim, right or option.

Zoning. The procedure that classifies properties for specific purposes: residential, commercial, industrial and so on.

Zoning map. A map showing the various zones of permitted land uses under a zoning ordinance.

Zoning ordinance. Legal regulations to implement a zoning plan to control the use and character of real estate.

INDEX